The USS Cairo

THE USS CAIRO

History and Artifacts of a Civil War Gunboat

Elizabeth Hoxie Joyner

Foreword by Margie Riddle Bearss

McFarland & Company, Inc., Publishers
Jefferson, North Carolina, and London

All photographs are by Ken Parks except those credited to the Archives of the Vicksburg National Military Park. All photographs courtesy Vicksburg National Military Park, United States Department of the Interior.

Library of Congress Cataloguing-in-Publication Data

Joyner, Elizabeth Hoxie, 1959–
    The USS Cairo : history and artifacts of a Civil War gunboat / Elizabeth Hoxie Joyner ; foreword by Margie Riddle Bearss.
        p.   cm.
    Includes bibliographical references and index.

    ISBN 0-7864-2257-2 (softcover : 50# alkaline paper)

    1. Cairo (Gunboat)   2. United States—History—Civil War, 1861–1865—Antiquities.   3. Material culture—United States—History—19th century.   4. Seafaring life—United States—History—19th century.   5. United States—History—Civil War, 1861–1865—Naval operations.   I. Title.
    E595.C3J69   2006
    973.7'58—dc22   2006010035

British Library cataloguing data are available

On the cover: The USS Cairo shortly after commissioning in 1862 (Archives of the Vicksburg National Military Park)

Manufactured in the United States of America

McFarland & Company, Inc., Publishers
    Box 611, Jefferson, North Carolina 28640
    www.mcfarlandpub.com

To Raymond and Travis

Acknowledgments

First and foremost, I thank God, from whom I have received many blessings.

I thank my loving and supportive husband, Raymond, who encouraged me to write this book and who put up with my odd working habits and the many late nights and extremely early hours when I was awake in order to work on this book.

I further wish to thank my wonderful son, Travis, who is developing a fascination with the Civil War and its naval history.

I am grateful to have been blessed with a father and mother who always provided much love and encouragement in helping me to fulfill my goals.

It is with grateful appreciation that I thank Mrs. Margie Bearss for her untiring efforts and careful attention in cataloging the hundreds of unique and fascinating artifacts that encompass the *Cairo* collection. In a conversation with Margie on a February afternoon in 2002, it was evident that her love for and fascination with the *Cairo* is just as strong today as it was back in 1960. She shared many wonderful stories about the days when the artifacts were being discovered.

I'd also like to acknowledge Mrs. Suzanne Banton for all of the efforts that she put forth on the initial cataloging of the *Cairo* artifacts.

Finally, I thank Mr. Ken Parks for all of his valuable assistance in the photo documentation of the *Cairo* collection. All of the photographs in this book were taken by Mr. Parks. They help to document the collection for present and future researchers who are curious about *Cairo* and the men who served aboard her. These photographs are now part of the archives of the Vicksburg National Military Park.

Contents

Acknowledgments vii

Foreword by Margie Riddle Bearss 1

Introduction 5

About the Catalog Numbers and Descriptions 19

1. Cannons and Ammunition Boxes 21

2. Small Arms and Equipment 43

3. Navigational Devices and Ship's Components 55

4. Furniture, Fixtures and Lighting 69

5. Cookware and Eating Utensils 83

6. Bottles 103

7. Clothing and Fabric 113

8. Personal Effects 135

9. Medical Equipment 173

10. Tools and Measuring Devices 181

Index 189

Foreword

by Margie Riddle Bearss

History leaves few time capsules, but those that exist are full of fascinating information. Excavated cities deserted over a period of years and falling gradually into decay have their stories to tell, but they do not offer the treasures we find in Pompeii. Covered in a short time by volcanic ash, that city was preserved almost intact, transferred into a time capsule that reveals the household activities and artifacts—both trivial and important—of a given moment in history.

Cairo is a time capsule, too. This Civil War gunboat was frozen in time a few minutes before noon on December 12, 1862.

Cairo went down 12 minutes after a torpedo exploded under the port bow. At the time of the explosion, *Cairo*'s crew and those of the other vessels had loaded and primed the big guns, preparing to open fire on the Confederates posted behind Benson Blake's levee and the Rebel gun emplacements that scarred Drumgould's Bluff. Fragments of Confederate shells from earlier engagements were lodged in the railroad iron armor.

Cairo's crew were at battle stations, so they wore their small arms—pistols, cutlasses and accoutrements. They carried their money on their persons. In the first frantic efforts to run the boat in to the river bank and secure it and a few minutes later after the cry "Abandon ship!" rang out, the men did not have time to rescue their personal possessions.

So *Cairo* sank with most of the sailors' gear just as they left it when they went to their battle stations—tiny vignettes of a sailor's life on a river gunboat.

1

The midday meal for the men was being kept warm on the galley stove. Beef bones in a large copper pot and a big bread pan in the oven remained after the salvage of the stove.

One sailor left his loaded pepperbox pistol hanging on a coat hook attached to a bulkhead. Nearby, nailed to the same bulkhead, was a glass photo in a lovely copper frame. Below this on the deck was a personal box containing sewing thread, needles and two pocket knives.

My husband, Ed Bearss, along with Don Jacks and Warren Grabau, discovered *Cairo* in 1956. At that time, nobody was in charge of the artifacts, so as a volunteer, I washed and tried to protect the relics. I spent several thousand hours (Ed estimates some 3,000) washing off mud, photographing, writing letters of inquiry to experts asking all sorts of questions, cataloging, treating and retreating. I was familiar with all of the relics and had been in close touch with the museum department of the National Park Service. When the Park Service gained title to *Cairo*, the Park Service gave me a contract to catalog the artifacts with drawings, photos, etc., which I did. I handled every relic twice—once when the relics were brought in from the river following their recovery, and again when the Park Service took over. I prepared some of the original catalog and the complete Park Service catalog.

The first artifact I saw from *Cairo* was in 1957. It was an iron pin driven into a piece of wood. This came from the top of the pilothouse. The wood was eroded badly. I held that in my hand, and I suppose it was then that I was lost. An all-consuming interest made me want to work on the artifacts—trying to protect and preserve them and to discover the facts surrounding their salvage, where each relic was found and what it was near. This has been an experience that I would not sell for millions of dollars.

I realized that given the speed with which the muddy artifacts were being brought in from the near-freezing river by the too-many volunteers who were helping, handling and cleaning, there was no way the items that told the story of *Cairo* and her crew's last minutes could be kept together. Then and there, I started trying to record as much as I could about where the artifacts came from and what they were found with. This was difficult. Salvage of the relics of the past was moving fast.

From the very first a great problem was people who wanted to wash and clean up everything. A glass negative that showed a man in uniform was washed clean before anyone could prevent it; through someone's good intentions, a photo that had meant much to a sailor was turned into a clear rectangle of glass.

Some of the volunteers saw bottles—whether medicine, condiment or beverage—as something to be washed sparkling clean. Often they threw away the shrinking, leaking cork and dumped the contents. At this point I obtained small sterile bottles, put small samples of medicines into them and sent them off to the state chemist for analysis. One apothecary jar of ointment, opened several days after salvage, had drops of mercury that had risen to the top. The analysis suggested that it was ointment for the treatment of syphilis.

Another volunteer worker, Vincent Canizaro, deserves much credit for his expert and painstaking cleaning and care of the guns and edged weapons—the personal pistols, artillery swords, razors and knives. The ones Vince cleaned still have the original blue on them. Cleaning by others was not always carefully done, and some weapons were left so that rust crept in.

One of the early divers, Ken Parks, was of invaluable help, telling me where various items were found and even drawing me sketches of a few areas.

Through the whole preservation effort runs the same thread: insufficient money to buy supplies needed, insufficient time of the volunteer workers to treat the artifacts properly, and above all an insufficient knowledge of what to do.

Many accounts of the sinking and salvage of *Cairo* have been written. Up until now the story of the artifacts has not been told except for a few articles like those found in *Life Magazine*, *Popular Mechanics* and several articles written by me in *Relics Magazine* and the *Antique Gun Magazine*.

I am very pleased that Elizabeth Joyner has taken on the difficult and challenging task of accounting for all these artifacts. I am also pleased and proud that she has let me help a little.

Introduction

The Civil War took place in the years 1861–1865. The grand Union strategy for winning the war was called the "Anaconda Plan." This plan, attributed to General Winfield Scott, proposed the strangling of the Confederacy by cutting it off from its external markets and sources of war materiel. Execution of this strategy by blockade of the southern coasts and control of the Mississippi River culminated in the surrender of Vicksburg on July 4, 1863. In order to fulfill this plan the Union needed gunboats and lots of them. That is where the story of *Cairo* begins.

James Buchanan Eads was a self-educated man who had made a fortune in salvaging cargoes from sunken boats on western rivers. Eads had strong convictions that the war could be won only through control of the Mississippi. This conviction coupled with a strong loyalty to the Union prompted him to put forth an effort to help the North win the war. He proposed to President Abraham Lincoln and his cabinet the conception of an inland navy.

He built, in five months' time, seven ironclads, *Cairo* being one of the seven. These ironclads, called so because of their iron covering, were also called "City Class."

Each vessel was named for cities along the upper Mississippi and Ohio rivers. *Cairo* was built in Mound City, Illinois, but named for Cairo, Illinois. Collectively, the seven were also referred to as Pook's Turtles, named so after their designer, Samuel Pook. Top speed for the ironclads was six knots. The seven were built specifically for river navigation; therefore they were designed with a flat bottom and a very shallow draft. Each vessel could float in as little as six feet of water.

Next came the tasks of manning these boats. *Cairo* had a total complement of 175 men—158 sailors and 17 officers. According to *Cairo*'s final muster, 43 percent of the crew were immigrants representing such countries as Ireland, England, Germany, Canada, Norway, Denmark, and France. Most of the crew had no prior naval training. They acquired the necessary skills of manning a gunboat as they went along. Backgrounds of the men varied. Some had previously been farmers who had just joined for the cause. Other occupations ranged from brewer to school teacher. But most simply listed their prior occupation as "none." The *Cairo*'s third and final commanding officer and the one most closely associated with *Cairo* was Lt. Commander Thomas O. Selfridge.

By the time that Selfridge came aboard *Cairo* to assume command, the men were so well trained that he mistakenly identified them as long-time veteran rivermen.

Daily routine for the crew began at the early hour of 0530, at which time the men would be awakened and told to "turn to." They would roll out of their hammocks, dress, roll and store their hammocks and report to the top deck or hurricane deck where they would store their hammocks and perform the morning ritual of scrubbing, swabbing, and holystoning the decks. Following this part of the morning's routine, the men would be given a brief time to clean and tidy themselves and get ready for inspection, which took place every morning to check for general bodily cleanliness. During one of these inspections, if a man was found to be unclean, the penalty was very heavy; on the night of his offense, his fellow crewmen would give him a sand bath using buckets of sand and scrub brushes. All the top layer of the crewman's skin would be scrubbed off. After undergoing such harsh treatment, the crewman would always be very sure to pass each morning's inspection by taking extra precautions to be clean.

Following inspection, the men's breakfast was served. This meal consisted of a hard biscuit (hardtack) and coffee. One sailor made the comment that the coffee was actually nothing more than hot, colored water facetiously called coffee. Meals aboard the gunboat were very bland, as evidenced by the number of condiment bottles (mustard and pepper bottles) found aboard *Cairo*. These meals consisted mainly of salted beef or pork with beans and occasional fresh meat. Sometimes the crew would catch fish to supplement these meals. Although the cook on board *Cairo* was French, he was by no means a gourmet chef.

The USS *Cairo* as she appeared shortly after her commissioning in 1862 (Archives of the Vicksburg National Military Park).

Drilling on the guns was a major portion of the day. Each gun required five to six men. Each man had his own tasks to perform, and the tasks had to be performed flawlessly. Much time was spent in drilling on the guns for the sake of speed but also for the sake of safety. Firing a gun could be as dangerous for the ones firing as for those being fired upon. An incorrectly fired gun could explode, injuring or even killing those around it. Commander Selfridge believed in drilling on the guns—so much so, in fact, that he would wake the crew up at all hours of the night to have gun drills so they would be prepared if they were suddenly fired upon.

Cairo was ordered to proceed to the Yazoo River to find and destroy torpedoes that the Confederates had planted in the water.

The Sinking

On the fateful day of December 12, 1862, shortly before noon, *Cairo* was traveling with a flotilla of other vessels in the Yazoo River on a special mission to find and destroy torpedoes that had been placed in the water by Confederates.

Cairo diver Ken Parks being lowered into the Yazoo River for an exploratory dive (Archives of the Vicksburg National Military Park).

Civil War torpedoes were more like today's mines. The type used to sink *Cairo* consisted of five-gallon glass jars called demijohns, filled with black powder and anchored to the bottom of the river. Attached was a waterproofed copper wire that ran from the torpedo to the shore. Confederates stood by to detonate the torpedoes when the approaching boats were within close range.

Cairo was traveling toward the rear of the flotilla when gunfire was heard toward the front. Lieutenant Commander Selfridge, believing that the flotilla was being fired upon, ordered *Cairo* to move toward the front to see if she could be of some assistance. Her paddlewheel had turned just barely a dozen revolutions when she was hit twice, in quick succession, by torpedoes. One hit an undetermined area of her starboard bow section. Another struck her port bow section, dislodging her number one port gun and leaving a gaping hole. *Cairo* went down in a matter of 12 minutes without any loss of life.

Present day site of the *Cairo*'s sinking on the Yazoo River.

Selfridge ordered the boat run aground in order to save it. He soon realized that his efforts were futile, and so he issued the command "Abandon ship!" Some of the crew used the *Cairo*'s launch and cutters to escape the sinking vessel, but most simply jumped through the gun ports and swam to shore.

The Confederates on the shore had not remained to take prisoners. *Queen of the West*, a ram traveling with *Cairo*, picked up the crew. The gunboat sank in six fathoms or 36 feet of water. Her chimneys were still protruding out of the water. To better conceal the location of the ironclad—since she sank so deeply in Confederate territory—the ram knocked her chimneys back into the river. Although several attempts were made by the North (at later dates) to raise the *Cairo*, none were ever successful. *Cairo* remained beneath the muddy waters of the Yazoo River, approximately eight miles north of Vicksburg, Mississippi.

Discovery and Salvage

Ninety-four years after her sinking, *Cairo* was located by Edwin Bearss (Vicksburg National Military Park historian), Don Jacks, and

Pilot house as it was being raised to the surface (Archives of the Vicksburg National Military Museum).

Warren Grabau. The three men had conducted research utilizing maps and charts of the area and had also talked with residents who told them that at times, when the river level was low, the pilot house could be seen just above the river's surface. In 1952, armed with a compass and using a small boat, the three men began to search for the sunken ironclad. The compass was placed in the bottom of the boat to get it as close to the river's bottom as possible. When the small boat traveled over the area where the vessel was thought to have

Front casemate as it was being raised (Archives of the Vicksburg National Military Museum).

sunk, the needle of the compass began to fluctuate wildly. The men later came back to the site with probes to outline the shape of the vessel. It was determined that this was indeed *Cairo*.

The wreck was raised by a private group of citizens who called their organization "Operation Cairo." The members of this group donated their time, money, and equipment to raise and preserve the ironclad and its artifacts.

People involved in the raising soon realized that this project was becoming more of a logging operation, thanks to the huge logs that had fallen all around and on top of *Cairo*. Before any actual raising of the vessel could take place, all of the logs had to be removed.

Cairo was finally brought up and placed on barges on December 12, 1964, exactly 102 years to the date of her sinking. At this time, Warren County (of which Vicksburg is the county seat) had ownership of *Cairo*, but because the county lacked the funding to restore it, ownership was eventually transferred to the state of Mississippi.

Divers were used to bring up some of the smaller artifacts found on board *Cairo*. The cannons were also brought up during this operation.

Although the plan was to raise *Cairo* intact, she was so heavy—even after crews blew all the mud and silt out—that she broke in half, falling back into the river. A decision was then made to cut her into three sections, salvaging as much as possible.

The vessel was taken to Pascagoula, Mississippi, to Ingalls Shipyard, where she remained for 13 years. While in Pascagoula, the *Cairo* was pieced back together. In an effort to preserve the wooden hull, a system of hoses was placed throughout the vessel. It was thought at the time that the best method of preserving the vessel was to periodically wet the wooden timbers of the hull. Actually, this did more harm than good, and as a result about 50 percent of the *Cairo*'s wood was lost.

Restoration

In 1973, the National Park Service gained title to *Cairo* and in 1977 brought the gunboat back, via barge, to her final resting place within Vicksburg National Military Park in Vicksburg, Mississippi.

Cairo was brought back to Vicksburg in large sections. The sections were then cut into smaller pieces and trucked to her present-day location. Today, *Cairo* rests just below the U.S. Navy Monument, about eight miles into the Vicksburg National Military Park tour route and just ahead of the entrance to Vicksburg National Cemetery.

Upon her arrival at Vicksburg National Military Park, *Cairo* was placed in a dry berth. A canopy was later constructed over the boat to protect it from the detrimental effects of the rain and sun.

Restoration was conducted by a special division of the National Park Service, Denver Service Center. Local experts in the fields of carpentry, welding, and painting were hired for the monumental task of restoring this vessel. Using a restoration method called "ghosting," crews connected all useable original sections of the vessel by "ghosting" framework that supported the original wood and filled in the missing pieces of the vessel.

USS *Cairo*: A Time Capsule of Life Aboard a Civil War Ironclad

When divers first entered *Cairo* she was like a time capsule. Many of her artifacts were perfectly preserved, found just as they had been left on that fateful day in December 1862.

Among divers' discoveries was a glass negative nailed to a bulkhead in a dark space too small for a man to stand. Hanging from a coat hook by its trigger guard was a small pistol. Beneath it was a personal chest containing a sewing kit, a hat ribbon (USS *Cairo* stamped on it), a handmade thread holder and some unidentifiable type of cloth. A sailor had his clothes in a wooden tub. Beside it was a large brush and some soap. Though some soap was salvaged in containers, this soap by the tub went to suds when the water from the hoses hit it. This sailor had tossed his shoes onto a pile of cannonballs.

One discovery "Operation Cairo" made was that the gunboat was not fitted out with regulation furniture. Instead it was furnished with a hodgepodge of regular household furnishings, not at all of the type one would expect. Very scattered portions of the furniture were recovered. The river was icy, the weather freezing. The vessel was unevenly set on the barge and there was constant danger of its slipping back into the current. So many more important-looking things than pieces

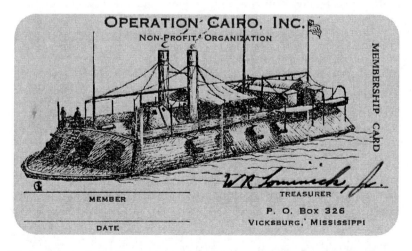

"Operation Cairo" card (Archives of the Vicksburg National Military Park).

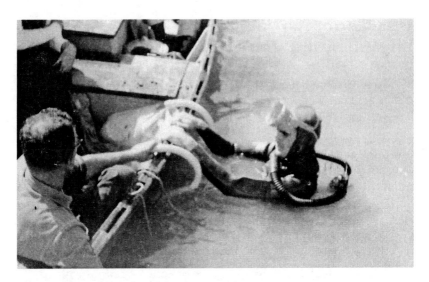

Cairo **diver Ken Parks (Archives of the Vicksburg National Military Museum).**

of furniture were scattered in the debris and mud, and so much was falling back into the river, that one can understand why broken chairs weren't salvaged.

Leather book covers, so thin that the leather had begun to curl before it was brought off the vessel, were found, revealing that *Cairo* had carried, at the least, two Holy Bibles (one from the London Bible Society) and one *Orrendorf French Grammar*. These did not preserve well. The spine from the French grammar book is on display at the Cairo Museum.

Cairo diver Ken Parks later commented that he and other divers developed eyeballs in the ends of their fingers, operating mainly by feel alone in the murky darkness of the Yazoo River.

One of Parks' scariest experiences was when he was trying to tie off the boat from which the divers were working. Since the current was so swift, he had to dive down onto the *Cairo* and take a piece of rebar or pipe and place it down inside of the pilot house to have something to tie the boat off. While he was doing this, something started nipping at his fingers. Unable to see his assailant, he shot out of the water like a rocket. If the boat from which he had dived had been directly overhead, he probably would have broken his neck. Fortunately, he was uninjured, but everyone on the shore got a good

Divers Ken Parks (back to camera) and Skeeter Hart (Archives of the Vicksburg National Military Museum).

laugh. A little while later, he went back down into the pilot house, and when the nibbling started again, he grabbed the culprit and brought it to the surface. It was river shrimp. The pilot house was full of them.

Low in the midsection magazine, amazingly, divers found that the Dahlgren shells were in a dry compartment. This particular compartment was lead lined and had kept the shells dry for a century.

During the years that *Cairo* was at Ingalls, the artifacts were kept at Vicksburg National Military Park. An artifacts committee was organized, made up of local citizens led by Margie Riddle Bearss. Working

Present day view of USS *Cairo*. Visible are her three bow guns—left to right, a 42-pounder (catalog number VICKC-2120), an 8 inch (catalog number VICKC-2122) and another 42-pounder (catalog number VICKC-2119).

in a Quonset hut equipped with only a few lights, a sink, and a couple of space heaters, this committee spent countless hours washing the mud from hundreds of articles until their hands turned blue from the cold. Margie then undertook the daunting task of identifying the hundreds of items. She conducted the first cataloging of these items. In some cases, Margie had to conduct extensive correspondence with pharmaceutical and other companies, historians and museum professionals in order to identify the objects and their contents.

It is these notes and records that form the basis for this book. Margie's well-defined and precise accounts of treatments and general notes on the artifacts have made this book possible. Written over 40 years ago, Margie's notes still provide much-needed information to researchers and curatorial staff who seek to learn more about these Civil War sailors and their life aboard this vessel.

One thing Margie especially remembers about the salvage oper-

Present day port side view featuring the *Cairo*'s pilot house (octagonal iron structure at top). Visible also are *Cairo*'s four port guns and carriages displayed on a reconstructed portion of the gundeck. Visitors to the site may board the vessel to get a close-up glimpse of this Civil War vessel's partially restored interior.

ation is the smells associated with the various artifacts. The first smell Margie noticed was from a can of talcum powder. Despite the deterioration of the tin after years underwater, the powder retained a scent of roses. Margie also recalls that the pepper scent was still so strong that it caused her to sneeze.

We have learned many things from examining the artifacts. These men of so long ago were not really all that different from people today.

Cairo gives us a remarkable picture of life aboard a Civil War gunboat, an image unmatched in its clarity.

Today, work is ongoing in order to preserve this unique Civil War vessel and her artifacts for all future generations.

The following pages contain descriptions, measurements and other details of the artifacts of the USS *Cairo*.

About the Catalog Numbers and Descriptions

When the *Cairo* artifacts began coming to the surface in 1957, Margie Riddle Bearss was instrumental in gathering and caring for them. As part of her efforts in recovery, cleaning, and storage, she kept extensive notes on the artifacts, and also completed the first cataloging, assigning a number to each item.

In 1973, the National Park Service gained title to the *Cairo*. Beginning in 1974 artifacts were assigned new catalog numbers and were catalogued by park service personnel, utilizing updated park service procedures. However, the original numbers, now known as "Bearss numbers," were also included in the records in order to provide access to Bearss' notes, which are held in the archives of the Vicksburg National Military Park. Any item cataloged by Margie Bearss still retains the Bearss number as part of its current catalog record.

The numbers visible in some of this book's photographs are Bearss numbers. The official Park Service catalog numbers, all beginning with VICKC-, are used in the text and captions.

The original catalog descriptions included measurements in feet and inches. The Park Service catalog descriptions use metric measurements. Because the descriptions in this book draw on both the Park Service cataloging and the earlier work, the reader will find both types of measurements used in the text.

1

CANNONS AND AMMUNITION BOXES

Cannons

The *Cairo's* 13 cannon tubes were all brought up before the vessel was salvaged. This was done to lighten the weight. The tubes brought up, in order of their raising, were:

- An 8-inch Navy gun with carriage, salvaged September 14, 1960 (at the time the pilot house was raised). It was loaded with canister and elevated by screw. This one was not treated for preservation like the rest. At the time the others were dipped in the oakite, this one was onboard the *Sprague*. It was hand scrubbed for rust in 1961.

- A 30-pdr Naval Parrott Rifle, salvaged October 20, 1963. This cannon had a wooden tompion in its muzzle. Contrary to regulations, it was also loaded with an explosive shell. Its factory number is NO. 61, and it was cast in 1862.

- A 32-pdr Smoothbore, salvaged October 20, 1963. It was the No. 3 starboard gun, and was brought up with its carriage. A quoin was lost in raising. This gun was not loaded; likely it had just been fired. It was No. 276.

- An 8-inch Navy gun, salvaged October 25, 1963. It was the middle bow gun, elevated by quoin. It was loaded with a double charge of grape. No. 368 was its factory number.

- A 42-pdr rifle (was originally smoothbore but had been rifled), salvaged October 27, 1963. It was the port bow gun, elevated by screw. It was loaded with explosive shell filled with shrapnel. Its carriage was brought up separately and had a broken wheel. No. 8 was its factory number.

- A 42-pdr rifle salvaged October 27, 1963, the starboard bow gun. It was elevated by a quoin. It was loaded with an 87-pound explosive shell.

- A 32-pdr smoothbore, salvaged October 27, 1963. It was the No. 1 port gun. It was double loaded with canister. Its carriage was brought up separately. Its tube was dismounted from the torpedo explosion because it was almost directly above the explosion. It was elevated by quoin. This tube had more corrosion on it than the others, and the muzzle is badly pitted.

- A 42-pdr rifle, salvaged October 31, 1963. It was the No. 1 starboard gun. Its carriage was brought up separately. It was loaded with an

87-pound explosive shell. In fact, it is still loaded with an explosive shell. This gun was cast in 1837. It was an "antique" even in 1862. It can be distinguished easily by the odd knob on the cascabel. It resembles a cup handle.

• An 8-inch Navy gun, salvaged November 6, 1963. It was the No. 3 port gun. It was loaded with grape. Its factory number was No. 358. It was elevated by quoin.

• A 32-pdr smoothbore, salvaged November 6, 1963. It was the No. 3 port gun. It was elevated by quoin. Its factory number was No. 284.

• A 32-pdr. smoothbore, salvaged November 1963. It was the No. 4 port gun. It came up with its carriage. It was elevated by quoin. It was loaded with a solid shot. This gun tube was cracked in several places, and bulges. This was done by the Navy demolition team when they used too much "shape" charge to unload it. Half of the severed solid shot also broken by the charge is in the museum. The other half is in the gun.

• A 32-pdr, salvaged November 6, 1963. It was the No. 4 starboard gun. It came up with its carriage. No. 226 is its number.

• A 32-pdr, salvaged November 6, 1963. It was the stern starboard gun. It came up with its carriage. No. 280 is its number.

A diagram on page 24 shows the location of each gun and its VICKC number.

PORT BOW CANNON

A 42-rifle made of Iron. Marks: right trunnion: K. & W./F.P.F. (cast at Fort Pitt Foundry, Pittsburgh, PA); right rimbase: 312; left trunnion: 1856; base of breech: 8359; muzzle face: No. 28/B.H.; top, between trunnions: U.S. Pitted but otherwise complete and in good condition. Tube length measures 3.302 m; bore diameter is 184 mm; trunnion diameter measures 178 mm. Catalog number **VICKC-2119** with carriage **VICKC-2134**.

PORT BOW CARRIAGE

Wood (white oak) with wood and iron fixtures (painted black); screw elevation system. Measurements (excluding wheels) L × W × H

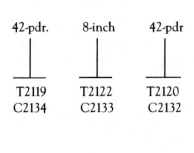

42-pdr.   8-inch   42-pdr

T2119   T2122   T2120
C2134   C2133   C2132

32-pdr ———| T2125   T2121 |——— 42-pdr.
          | C2135   C2144 |

8-inch ———| T2124   T2123 |——— 8-inch
          | C2136   C2143 |

32-pdr. ———| T2126   T2128 |——— 32-pdr.
           | C2137   C2142 |

32-pdr. ———| T2127   T2129 |——— 32-pdr.
           | C2138   C2141 |

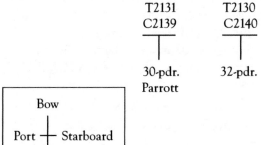

T2131   T2130
C2139   C2140

30-pdr.   32-pdr.
Parrott

Bow
Port + Starboard
Stern

1.867 m × 978 mm × .686 mm; wheel radius measures 102 mm. Slightly checked. Right front wheel missing. Right key missing from chain. Screw handle missing. Left cap square is catalog number **VICKC-1988**. Right cap square is catalog number **VICKC-1980**. Carriage catalog number **VICKC-2134** with tube **VICKC-2119**.

CENTER BOW CANNON

8-inch smoothbore. Iron. Marks: right trunnion: 8 IN/1845; left trunnion: P./G.A.M.; base ring periphery: F.P.F. (Fort Pitt Foundry, Pittsburgh, PA) NO 368 64.0.26. Measurements include: tube length: 3.048 m; bore diameter: 213 mm; trunnion diameter: 178 mm. Pitted, but complete and in good condition. Loaded with grape. Raised 25 Oct. 1963. Cannon catalog number **VICKC-2122** with carriage **VICKC-2133**.

CENTER BOW CARRIAGE

Wood (white oak) with wood and iron fixtures (painted black); quoin elevation system. Right cap square is catalog number 1979. Known old catalog numbers for fixtures: left front wheel: 4434; right front wheel: 4107; left rear wheel: 4596; right rear wheel: 4103; bed: 6531. Measurements (excluding wheels) L × W × H are 1.581 m × 949 mm × 660 mm; wheel radius: 102 mm. Carriage is incomplete, but in good condition. Right chain is missing. Handle is broken off quoin. Carriage catalog number **VICKC-2133** with cannon **VICKC-2122**.

STARBOARD BOW CANNON

Iron rifled. Marks: right trunnion: K. & W./F.P.F. (Fort Pitt Foundry, Pittsburgh, PA); right rimbase: 324; left trunnion: 1856; base of breech: 8397; muzzle face: No 20/B.H.; top, between trunnions: U.S. Measurements: tube length: 3.302 m; bore diameter: 184 mm; trunnion diameter: 178 mm. Gun is complete and in good

Opposite: Diagram of gun placement on the *Cairo*. The "T" number is the VICKC catalog number for the gun's tube. The "C" number is for the carriage.

No. 1 starboard cannon—forward view of gun (VICKC-2121) and carriage (VICKC-2144).

condition but exhibiting some pitting. Raised October 27, 1963. Catalog number **VICKC-2120** with carriage **VICKC-2132**.

STARBOARD BOW CARRIAGE

Wood (white oak) with wood and iron fixtures (painted black); quoin elevation system. Right cap square is catalog number 1981. Known old catalog numbers for fixtures: left front wheel: 4039; right rear wheel: 4032; bed: 5374. Measurements: L × W × H (excluding

wheels): 1.866 m × 977 mm × 711 mm; radius of wheels: 102 mm. Carriage is incomplete but in good condition although slightly checked. Right front and left rear axle tree bands missing. Right chain and key missing. Right side-shackle and pin missing. Left side tackle eye bolt missing. Catalog number **VICKC-2132** with cannon **VICKC-2120**.

NO. 1 STARBOARD CANNON

Iron. Rifled Marks: right trunnion: J. M./ C.F. (Columbia Foundry, Georgetown, D.C.); left trunnion: 1837; base of breech: 8620; muzzle face: No 26; top, between trunnions: U.S. Measurements: Tube length:

No. 1 starboard cannon—rear view of gun (VICKC-2121) and carriage (VICKC-2144).

3.302 m. Bore diameter: 184 mm; trunnion diameter: 178 mm. Incomplete but in good condition exhibiting some pitting. Raised October 31, 1963. Catalog number **VICKC-2121** with carriage **VICKC-2144**.

No. 1 Starboard Carriage

Wood (white oak) with wood and iron fixtures (painted black); quoin elevation system. Left cap square catalog number: 1984. Known old catalog numbers for fixtures: left front wheel: 4177; right front wheel: 4178; left rear wheel: 4591; quoin has only "65" legible. Measurements: L × W × H (excluding wheels): 1.867 m × 984 mm × 692 mm. Incomplete but in good condition. Slightly checked. Handle broken off quoin. Bed is split up the middle. Wheel pins missing. Catalog number **VICKC-2144** with cannon **VICKC-2121**.

No. 2 Starboard Cannon

Iron. Smoothbore. Marks: right trunnion: 8 IN./1845; left trunnion: P./G.A.M.; base ring periphery: F.P.F. (Fort Pitt Foundry, Pittsburgh, PA) No 348 64.0.8. Measurements: tube length: 3.048 m.; bore diameter: 213 mm; trunnion diameter: 178 mm. In complete but good condition exhibiting some pitting. Raised September 14, 1960. Catalog number **VICKC-2123** with (Reproduction carriage) **VICKC-2143**.

No. 2 Starboard Carriage (Reproduction)

Wood (yellow pine). Measurements: L × W × H (excluding wheels): 1.854 m × 997 mm × 279 mm; radius of wheels: 108 mm. In complete/excellent condition. Constructed in 1983 by National Park Service Denver Service Center personnel at restoration shop for USS *Cairo*. Catalog number **VICKC-2143** with cannon **VICKC-2123**.

No. 3 Starboard Cannon

Iron. Smoothbore. Marks: right trunnion: 32/1845; left trunnion: P./S.B.; base ring periphery: W.P.F.A. (West Point Foundry, Cold Springs, NY) No. 276 42.2.21; atop breeching rope clevis: 777. Measurements: tube length: 2.6924 m; bore diameter: 160 mm; trun-

The starboard side of the *Cairo* retains its original iron plating. Protruding through the gunports are the number 3 gun (catalog number VICKC-2128) and the number 4 gun (catalog number VICKC-2129). Both are 32-pounders.

Close-up of *Cairo*'s number 4 starboard gun, a 32-pounder (catalog number VICKC-2129). Starboard side of vessel is displayed with its original 2½ inch thick iron plating.

nion diameter: 162 mm. Complete and in good condition exhibiting some pitting. Raised October 20, 1963. Catalog number **VICKC-2128** with carriage **VICKC-2142**.

No. 3 Starboard Carriage

Wood (white oak) with wood and iron fixtures (painted black); quoin elevation system. Left cap square catalog number **VICKC-1972**. Measurements: L × W × H (excluding wheels): 1.486 m × 899 mm × 610 mm. Complete and good condition exhibiting some slight checking. Catalog number **VICKC-2142** with cannon **VICKC-2128**.

No. 4 Starboard Cannon

Iron. Smoothbore. Marks: right trunnion: 32/1845; left trunnion: P./A.S.W. (Fort Pitt Foundry, Pittsburgh, PA); base ring periphery: F.P.F. No. 226 42.2.20. Measurements: tube length: 2.6924 m; bore diameter: 160 mm; diameter of trunnions: 162 mm. In complete and good condition exhibiting some pitting. Raised November 6, 1963. Catalog number **VICKC-2129** with carriage **VICKC-2141**.

No. 4 Starboard Carriage

Wood (white oak) with wood and iron fixtures (painted black); quoin elevation system. Right cap square catalog number **VICKC-1974**. Measurements: L × W × H (excluding wheels): 1.486 m × 870 mm × 610 mm; radius of wheels: 95 mm. Incomplete but in good condition. Exhibiting some slight checking. Right rear cap square bolt missing. Catalog number **VICKC-2141** with cannon **VICKC-2129**.

Stern Starboard Cannon

Iron. Smoothbore. Marks: right trunnion: 32/1845; left trunnion: P./S.B.; base ring periphery: W.P.F.A. (West Point Foundry, Cold Springs, NY) No. 280 42.2.7.; atop breeching rope clevis: 796. Measuring: tube length: 2.6924 m; bore diameter: 160 mm; diameter of trunnions: 162 mm. In complete and good condition but exhibiting some pitting. Raised November 6, 1963. Catalog number **VICKC-2130** and with carriage catalog number **VICKC-2140**.

STERN STARBOARD CARRIAGE

Wood (white oak) with wood and iron fixtures (painted black); screw elevation system. Cap square catalog number **VICKC-1983**. Measuring: L × W × H (excluding wheels): 1.581 m × 946 mm × 737 mm; radius of wheel: 102 mm. Carriage is incomplete but in good condition with slight checking. Axle rings missing. Catalog number **VICKC-2140** and with cannon **VICKC-2130**.

STERN (AFT) PORT CANNON

Iron. Rifled. Marks: right trunnion: 1862/30 PDR/4.2; left trunnion: P.; base ring periphery: R.P.P. N 61 3460 LBS; right rimbase periphery behind rear sight: 61; Made at West Point Foundry, Cold Springs, NY. Measurements: tube length: 2.870 m; bore diameter: 108 mm; diameter of trunnions: 133 mm. In complete and good condition exhibiting some pitting. Raised October 20, 1963. Catalog number **VICKC-2131** with carriage **VICKC-2139**.

STERN (AFT) PORT CARRIAGE

Wood (white oak) with wood and iron fixtures (painted black); quoin elevation system. Right cap square is catalog number **VICKC-1975**. Measuring: L × W × H (excluding wheels): 1.486 × 895 mm × 622 mm; radius of wheels: 102 mm. In complete and good condition. Slightly checked. Catalog number **VICKC-2139** with cannon catalog number **VICKC-2131**.

NO. 4 PORT CANNON

Iron. Smoothbore. Marks: right trunnion: 32/1845; Left trunnion: P./A.S.W.; base rign periphery: F.P.P.(?) No. 230 42.1.18. (Fort Pitt Foundry, Pittsburgh, PA). Measurements: tube length: 2.6924 m; bore diameter: 160 mm; diameter of trunnions: 162 mm. In complete and good condition. Pitted. Raised November 6, 1963; loaded with solid shot. Broken by Navy demolition team when unloading it. Mark "F.P.P." might be "F.P.F." Catalog number **VICKC-2127** with carriage catalog number **VICKC-2138**.

Stern (Aft) Port cannon (VICKC-2131) and carriage (VICKC-2139). 30 PDR Parrott.

No. 4 Port Carriage

Wood (white oak) with wood and iron fixtures (painted black); quoin elevation system. Left cap square is catalog number **VICKC-1969**; right cap square is catalog number **VICKC-1970**. Measuring: L × W × H (excluding wheels): 1.492 m × 895 mm × 616 mm; radius of wheels: 102 mm. Incomplete/Good. Slightly checked. Left key is missing. Right chain and key missing. Carriage is catalog number **VICKC-2138** and with tube **VICKC-2127**.

No. 3 Port Cannon

Iron. Smoothbore. Marks: right trunnion: 32/1845; left trunnion: P.S.S.; base ring periphery: W.P.F.A. (West Point Foundry, Cold Springs, NY) No. 284 42.2.7.; atop breeching rope clevis: 790. Measuring: tube length: 2.6924 m; bore diameter: 160 mm; diameter of trunnions: 162 mm. In complete and good condition exhibiting some pitting. Raised November 6, 1963. Catalog number **VICKC-2126** with carriage catalog number **VICKC-2137**.

No. 3 Port Carriage

Wood (white oak) with wood and iron fixtures (painted black); quoin elevation system. Left cap square is catalog number **VICKC-1978**; right cap square is number **VICKC-1971**. Measuring: L × W × H (excluding wheels): 1.489 m × 889 mm × 603 mm; radius of wheels: 102 mm. Incomplete but in good condition, exhibiting slight checking. Gouge in left cheek. Right key missing from chain. Catalog number **VICKC-2137** with tube catalog number **VICKC-2126**.

No. 2 Port Cannon

Iron. Smoothbore: Marks: right trunnion: 8 IN./1845.; left trunnion: P./S.B.; base ring periphery: No. 358 63.0.18. Cast at the West Point Foundry in Cold Springs, NY. Measuring: tube length: 3.048 m; bore diameter: 213 mm, Diameter of Trunnions: 178 mm. In complete and good condition exhibiting some pitting. Raised November 3, 1963. Catalog number **VICKC-2124** with carriage catalog number **VICKC-2136**.

Port side featuring close-up view of number 1 gun, a 32-pounder (catalog number VICKC-2125), and number 2 port gun, an 8-inch (catalog number VICKC-2124).

NO. 2 PORT CARRIAGE

Wood (white oak) with wood and iron fixtures (painted black); screw elevation system. Left cap square is catalog number **VICKC-1987**; right cap square is number **VICKC-1982**. Measuring: L × W × H (excluding wheels): 1.866 m × 972 mm × 686mm; radius of wheels: 102 mm. Incomplete but good condition with slight checking. Part of elevating screw missing. Catalog number **VICKC-2136** with tube **VICKC-2124**.

NO. 1 PORT CANNON

Iron. Smoothbore: Marks: right trunnion: 32/1845; left trunnion: P./S.B.; base ring periphery: W.P.F.A. (West Point Foundry, Cold Springs, NY) No. 283 42.1.11. Measuring: tube length: 2.6924 m; bore diameter: 160 mm; diameter of trunnions: 162 mm. In com-

No. 1 port cannon. *Above, left:* Forward view of gun (VICKC-2125) and carriage (VICKC-2135). *Right:* Rear view of gun and carriage.

plete and good condition exhibiting pitting. Gun was dismounted by torpedo explosion which sank *Cairo*. Raised October 27, 1963. Tube was dismounted from torpedo explosion, wedged muzzle up into the gun port. Catalog number **VICKC-2125** with carriage catalog number **VICKC-2135**.

NO. 1 PORT CARRIAGE

Wood (white oak) with wood and iron fixtures (painted black); quoin elevation system. Left cap square is catalog number **VICKC-1973**. Right cap square bears marks IVXX. Measuring: L × W × H (excluding wheels): 1.473 m × 914 mm × 616 mm; radius of wheels: 108 mm. Incomplete, but in good condition. Wood slightly checked. On left, key and all but one link of chain missing; on right, key chain

Firing mechanism. VICKC-4373.

not connected to hook. Carriage's right cap square (catalog number **VICKC-1968**) broken by torpedo explosion which sank *Cairo*. Catalog number **VICKC-2135** with tube catalog number **VICKC-2125**.

FIRING MECHANISM

Two attached brass parts. One piece is 12 cm in length with an iron peg at the free end. A 1.1-cm-diameter hole in the attachment area. This section is attached to the other piece by a 1-cm-diameter screw. The second piece is 16 cm long with two 1-cm-diameter holes in boot. Two 1.5-cm-long brass screws on eyelets attached. Measuring: Length: 12 cm; hole diameter: 1.1 cm; Length: 16 cm. Incomplete but excellent condition. Catalog number **VICKC-4373**.

FIRING MECHANISM

Iron is oxidized; brass is clean, no tarnish. Two pieces, held together at joint by a screw: Diameter: 1 cm. One section length: 12.5

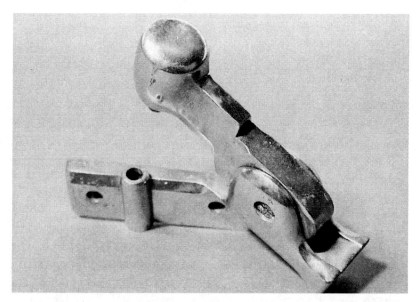

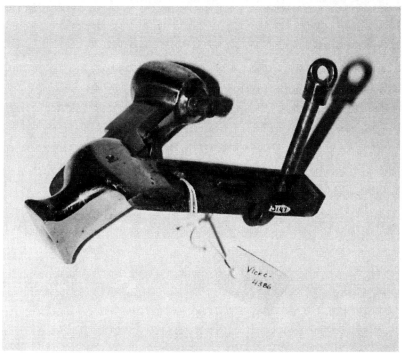

Firing mechanism. VICKC-4386.

cm; has iron peg: length: 1.3 cm; hole diameter is 1 cm. Drilled near attachment point. Other portion is 16 mm long; has 1-cm-diameter hole; 4.2 cm long. Second piece has 1-cm-diameter holes. One hole has 7.8 cm iron bolt and 1.5 cm screw on brass eyelet. Mea-

Military sight. VICKC-4377. Bearss number 2758.

suring: (1) section length: 12.5 cm; iron peg length: 1.3 cm. In complete and excellent condition. Catalog number **VICKC-4386.**

MILITARY SIGHT

Brass rectangular base with slightly arched base (to accommodate attachment to barrel of gun). Diameter (of round base) 9.5 cm (tapers to) 1.8 cm at lip on either side of sight shaft, with deep circular grooves; 2 mm greater diameter around them, suggesting screws with 1.2 cm diameter head were used to affix this item to barrel. Measuring: diameter (round base): 9.5 cm (tapers to) 1.8 cm at lip In complete and excellent condition. Catalog number **VICKC-4377.** Bearss number 2758.

DIRECT SIGHTING BAR

A long, hollow brass tube is mounted on a long four-sided wooden base. A brass tab at each end of tube has a screw through it to attach tube to base. Also a brass strap is mounted over the tube at the center and screws down on each side. Tube has no marking on it. Wood is black, very hard. Tube is mounted on top. Top is narrow and flat. Sides are slanted. Three horizontal slots near bottom of base. Wider end has "32/226" cut into the wood. Opposite end has a pin sticking out. Bottom is slightly concave. Metal pin near one end. Mea-

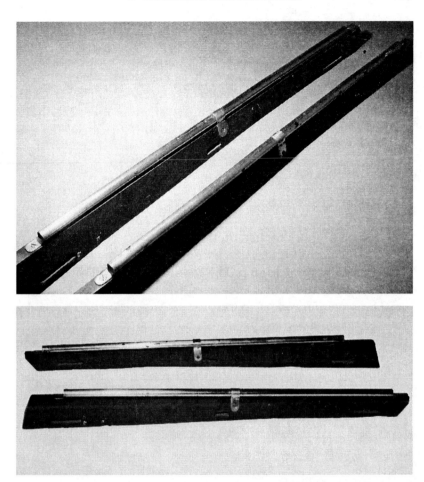

Direct sighting bars. VICKC-1468 and VICKC-1469.

suring: Length of base: 26¾" (679 mm); width of base: 1⅝" (41.3 mm)—1¹⁵⁄₁₆" (33.3 mm); length of tube: 22½" (572 mm) not including tabs. In complete but fair condition. Catalog number **VICKC-1468**.

DIRECT SIGHTING BAR

A long hollow brass tube is mounted on a long four-sided wooden base. A brass tab at each end of the tube has a screw through it to attach tube to base. Also a brass strap is mounted over the tube at the center and screws down on each side. Tube has 2 faint rings in brass near one end. Wood is black, very hard. Tube is mounted on the top which is narrow and flat. Sides are slanted. Three horizontal slots near bottom of base. Wider end has "32/230" cut into the wood. Opposite end has a pin sticking out. Bottom is slightly concave. Metal pin near one end. Measuring: length of base: 26¹³⁄₁₆" (681 mm); width of base: 1½" (38.1 mm)—1⅞" (47.6 mm); length of tube: 22½" (572 mm) excluding tabs. In complete but fair condition. Catalog number **VICKC-1469.**

Ammunition Boxes

A large number of ammunition boxes were recovered. Many, many ammunition box fragments were also found. Ammunition boxes often had red or white paint on the ends to denote explosive or solid shot.

Many of the wooden boxes were steam cleaned. This easily removed the mud and silt but also removed paint and lettering.

Polyethylene glycol was used as a preservative for many of the artifacts, including many of the wooden objects. One side effect of this chemical was that it darkened the wood and blurred the lettering.

The photograph at left shows an ammunition box fragment still retaining its original red paint and stenciled numbers.

Ammunition box fragment, VICKC-3999.

AMMUNITION BOX FRAGMENT

Square wood ammunition box top. Top surface painted red. Stenciled black letters read 5" 42 PDR. Four screw holes through fragment (one midway along each edge). One broken out to edge. Two small nail holes on opposing edges. Wood is "oily" (preservative?). Soft corners slightly shrunken and checked. Debris adheres. Leaching.

Unpainted surface contains large hole (4 cm in diameter, 1 cm deep) in center. Dark staining. Fragment is in fair condition.

8-Inch Navy Shell Ammunition Box

Large, heavy wooden box. Empty. No lid extant. Stenciled in black lettering on one end is: "CA ‑‑‑ ..../ U. S N / ST L ‑‑‑ IS/MO/." Some of the lettering very faint. According to the original catalog it read: "CAIRO GB/USN/ST. LOUIS/MO./." Stencil was put on upside down. Sides are nailed to the ends with 4 nails. Bottom nailed on with 3 nails into each end and 2 through each side. Two opposite sides have handles cut into them. Wood is comparatively light in color, and is soft. A few minor splits in the wood. Measuring: thickness: 1¹⁄₁₆" (27.0 mm); width: 10" (254 mm); length: 10" (254 mm); height: 10¼" (260 mm). In good condition. Catalog number **VICKC-667**.

8-Inch Navy Shell Ammunition Box

Top, bottom, two end pieces and one side of a heavy wooden box. Empty. Original catalog states this was a box for 8-inch Navy ammunition. Handle cut into one side. Red paint on the top. Top screwed on with large screw on each side. Two screws missing. One

Left: 8-inch Navy shell ammunition box (end view). *Right:* Top view of 8-inch Navy shell ammunition box. VICKC-667.

8-inch Navy shell ammunition box. VICKC-642.

32 PDR shell ammunition box. VICKC-675.

on an edge which is broken off. Four nails through sides to hold ends. Bottom held on by 3 nails into ends and 2 through the side. End pieces and bottom are rough. One end split near top. Some other splitting of wood at the nails. Wood is dark and fairly soft. Measuring: thickness 25.4 mm; width: 241.0 mm; length: 254.0 mm; height: 292.0 mm. Box is incomplete but in fair condition. Catalog number **VICKC-642**.

32 PDR SHELL AMMUNITION BOX

Small heavy wooden box. Empty. No lid extant. No lettering. Sides are nailed on the ends with 4 nails. Bottom nailed on with 3 nails into each end and 2 through each side. Two opposite sides have handle holds cut out of them. Wood fairly dark, somewhat soft. Box is solid with few splits or other damage. Scratch on one end. Nails sunken. Measuring: Thickness: 1³⁄₁₆" (30.2 mm); width: 8½" (216 mm); length: 8½" (216 mm); height: 8⅜" (213 mm). Good condition. Catalog number **VICKC-675**.

2

SMALL ARMS AND EQUIPMENT

The small arms were carefully and expertly cleaned by a local jeweler in Vicksburg. He worked on them a few at a time.

The muskets came up in poor condition. They were eroded; the ends of the barrels of several were completely gone.

The divers stated that if a musket was found standing on its butt with the muzzle up, the end of the muzzle was eroded. If the musket had fallen out of the rack and was lying flat on the gun deck, it was in much better shape. One had the bayonet in its reversed position.

MUSKET

Listed as Model 1816 U.S. Flintlock Musket. Converted to percussion, Belgian alteration. Musket is a .69 caliber smoothbore. Rear of lockplate marked "1833" (?) over "Midd, Conn." Lock marking in center of American eagle motif. "US." above and "Johnson" (in an arc) below. Printing "1833" behind nipple. Barrel is marked with initials "N W P" over a "P." (Nahum W. Patch was an inspector from 1831–49.) Some lettering partly obliterated. All parts present, includ-

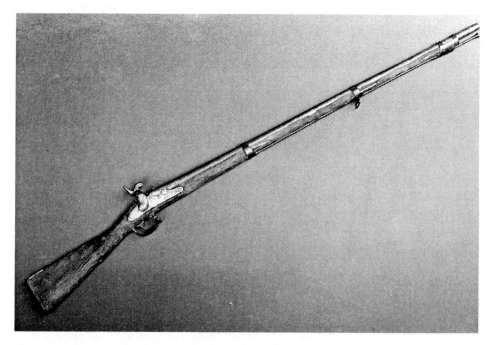

Musket. VICKC-1440.

Musket (close up view of lockplate). VICKC-1441.

ing ramrod. Hammer movable. Wood cracked, eroded. Measuring: barrel length: 1.067 m. Musket incomplete but in fair condition. Catalog number **VICKC-1440**.

Musket

Listed as Model 1816 U.S. Flintlock Musket. Converted to percussion, Belgian alteration. Musket is a .69 caliber smoothbore. Contract by A. Waters, Jr. Third type Waters. Center of lockplate stamped "Mill__" and "183_" (1834?). Barrel marked with "US" over "A" over "P" (?). Illegible due to rust. Also, "1834" (?) stamped behind nipple. Musket complete and in fair condition. Measuring: barrel length: 1.067 m. Catalog number **VICKC-1441**.

Musket

Model 1816 U.S. Flintlock Musket, converted to percussion, Belgian alteration. Musket is a .69 caliber smoothbore. Arms contract by A. Waters, Jr. Third type Waters. Center of lockplate marked "US" over "A Waters." Rear lockplate vertically stamped "Millsu_" and "1835." Barrel marked "US" over "TW." Also, "1835" stamped behind nipple. Muzzle barrel band, two bandsprings gone. One barrel band rusted apart, loose on barrel. Ramrod head, end of barrel rusted away. Measuring: barrel length: 1.016 m. Musket incomplete but in fair condition. Catalog number **VICKC-1442**.

REVOLVER

Colt 1849 Pocket Revolver. Six shot. Octagonal barrel. On left side of frame is printed "Colts Patent." Serial number "75447" printed in 4 places. Walnut grip, brass trigger guard. Brass back-strap down

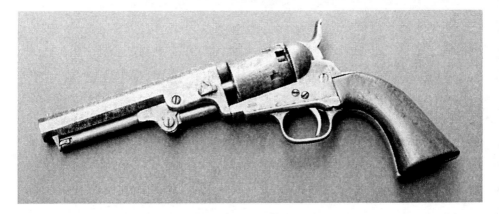

Revolver. VICKC-1231.

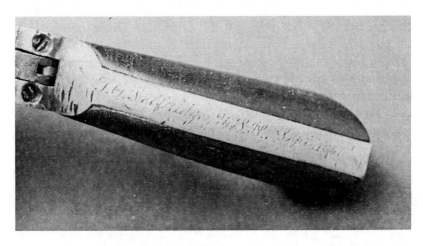

Revolver (back of grip—inscription). VICKC-1231.

back of grip has "T.O. Selfridge, U.S.N., Sept." inscribed on it in fancy script. Slightly worn. Constructed of walnut and brass. Measuring: length: 9⅞". Revolver is complete and in good condition. Catalog number **VICKC-1231**.

This revolver has functional moving parts. It belonged to *Cairo*'s third and final captain, Lieutenant Commander Thomas Oliver Selfridge.

PISTOL

Bar hammer, single-shot percussion pistol, .36 caliber, double action. Engraved frame. Now dark, uneven coloration, badly pitted, especially on right side. First 2¾₁₆" of barrel octagonal; end is round. Barrel is dark gray-black with some pitting. Pistol is complete and in good condition. Walnut grips "new." Oval trigger guard (pitted). Hammer, trigger movable. Marking: "Allens Patent" left side of hammer; "Allen" (Thurber?) on top of barrel; "2...2....2" on bottom of barrel. Measuring: length: 210 mm. Catalog number **VICKC-1434**.

Pistol. VICKC-1434.

REVOLVER

Lefaucheux Pinfire 12 mm. Six cartridge chambers. Ferrous metal; has rusted, been cleaned, now slightly rusty again. Surface lightly pitted. Grip is gone, part of hammer broken off, cylinder found near *Cairo* raising site in 1965. Donated by finder. Measuring: length: 238 mm; cylinder diameter: 41.3 mm. Catalog number **VICKC-1418**.

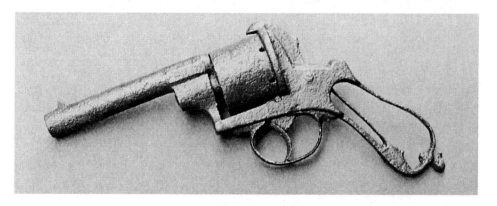

Revolver. VICKC-1418.

PISTOL (PEPPERBOX)

Allen and Wheelock Pepperbox Pistol. Six shot, .31 caliber, double action. Fired by bar hammer which has small number "8" on underside. Engraved frame, engraved cap shield fitted around base of

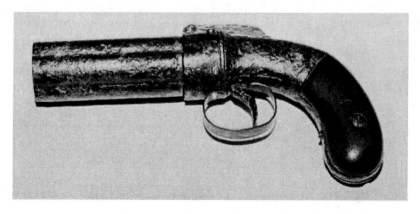

Pistol (pepperbox). VICKC-1419.

barrels over percussion nipples. Only traces of engraving evident. All ferrous metal parts pitted. Very little original finish left, and that is uneven, dull. Pistol is complete but in fair condition. Measuring: length: 175 mm; barrel diameter: 31.8 mm. Catalog number **VICKC-1419.**

PISTOL

Underhammer "Boot" pistol, .36 caliber. Heavy octagonal barrel. Some engraving still evident. Metal is an uneven, shiny, dark gray/black color with some pitting. Much original finish gone. Firing system is underhammer percussion type. Straight trigger, no guard. Sights are open-notch type. One at end of barrel is brass. Found with no handle. Two-inch brass backstrap on handle back is original. Pistol is incomplete but in good condition. Measuring: Length: 210 mm; barrel diameter: 23.8 mm. Four small holes in small brass piece around hammer bottom; "JR" in decorative mark top of barrel. Catalog number **VICKC-1435.**

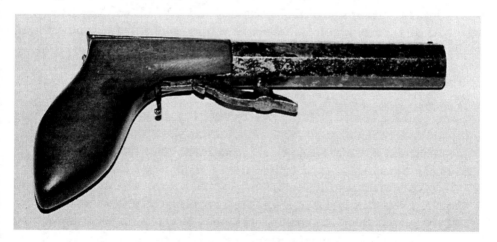

Pistol. VICKC-1435.

REVOLVER

Colt Model 1860 Army Revolver. Standard round cylinder Army variation, 6-shot rebated cylinder, .44 caliber. Cylinder roll engraved with naval engagement scene. Army-size grip, one-piece walnut. Blued

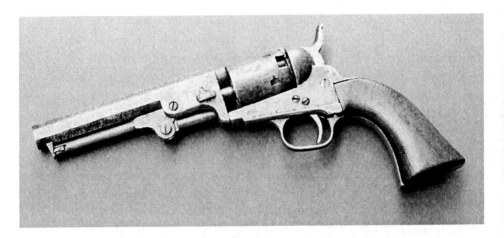

Revolver. VICKC-1444.

steel backstrap, brass trigger guard. Four screw type frame. Recoil shield cut for attachment of shoulder stock. Barrel marked "....col.... new," and "16408" stamped on trigger guard, other parts. "Colts patent" on left side of frame cylinder) and "_LTS Patent No 16408" over "Pat Sept 10th 1850" (?). Revolver is incomplete but in good condition. Measuring: barrel: 203 mm. Catalog number **VICKC-1444.**

REVOLVER

Colt Model 1860 Army Revolver, .44 caliber, six-shot rebated cylinder. Standard round cylinder Army variation. Cylinder roll engraved with naval engagement scene. Army-size grip, one-piece walnut. Blued steel backstrap, brass trigger guard. Four screw type frame. Recoil shield out for attachment of shoulder stock. Barrel marking: "A_Dress Co.. Sam CO_EW...Rica." Serial No. "17092" stamped on trigger guard, other parts. "Colts Patent" on side of frame. Revolver is incomplete but in good condition. Measuring: barrel length: 203 mm. Catalog number **VICKC 1443.**

FRICTION PRIMER BOX

Rectangular box made of tinned iron. Top edge is turned down over a concealed wire rim. Sides made of one piece. Top and bottom made separately. Top is hinged at the back. Two metal tabs (inside) form the hinges. Primer box is incomplete but in fair condition. Inside a raised oval rim on the top is printed in raised letters "FRICTION TUBES/100" and an illegible line of print. According to original catalog, "1861" was printed at bottom but this is no longer legible. Tin is shiny on the inside. On outside traces of the original black paint remain. Measuring: length: 4⅛";

Friction primer box. VICKC-1412.

width: 2⅜"; height: 2⁵⁄₁₆". Catalog number **VICKC-1412.**

Friction Primer

Made of two small brass tubes fitted together. At the top the tube extends out 9.53 mm from the long tube at a right angle. The end is flattened together. Extending out the opposite side of the long tube is a twisted wire which forms a loop at the end to receive the hook of the lanyard. The wire loop is bent parallel to the long tube. Inside has some dirt. Tarnished. Traces of a purple substance. Primer is complete but in fair condition. Measuring: length: 46 mm; diameter (of bottom of long tube): 4.76 mm. Catalog number **VICKC-956.**

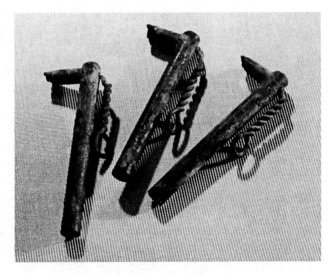

Friction primers—VICKC-956.

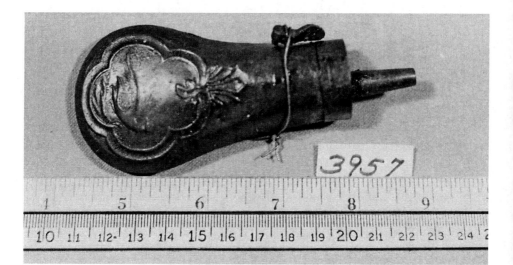

Priming flask. VICKC-1238.

PRIMING FLASK

Pistol flask(?) made of brass in two halves. Quite small. On one side in relief is a large bird with a fancy scalloped border. On opposite side is the same design but there is an irregular hole damaging most of the bird. A round cap on the top has a cone-shaped (nozzle?) spout. A small hole in the top. Wired on is a small tab-like device. Flask is complete but in fair condition. Brass is very tarnished, now dark brown. Greasy. Measuring: length: 4⅝", diameter of top: 1¹/₁₆"; maximum thickness: ¹⁵/₁₆". Catalog number **VICKC-1238.**

POWDER FLASK

Civilian. Made of brass. Main part has fancy raised ridge design along bottom on each side. Small ring, one near top and one near bottom, on each side. One has a small ferrous metal ring in it. Manufacturer's mark(?) stamped near top, four small marks with a symbol in each. Spout has graduated slot. Stamped on spout is "DIXON & SON." Thumb lever on top. Flask is complete and in good condition. Brass shiny. One spot in brass near one bottom ring. Measuring: total length: 7⅞"; diameter of top of flask: 1⅜". Catalog number **VICKC-1448.**

Powder flask. VICKC-1448. Bearss number 3946.

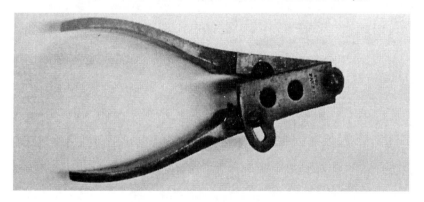

Bullet mold. VICKC-1242.

BULLET MOLD

For Colt .44. Made of ferrous metal. Two arms pivot at the top. Top parts of arms are flat, rectangular shape. Handles are curved. Inside has a hollow space, half on each side, in shape of ball and Minie ball. An extra plate is added on the top with two small holes in it. Above the holes is imprinted "Colts Patent." Below is a screw in an oval-shaped hole. At the top edge of one arm is "14 H" and a "T" near middle. Mold is complete and in good condition. Measuring: length: 127 mm; width: 30.2 mm; thickness: 27 mm. Catalog number **VICKC-1242.**

3

NAVIGATIONAL DEVICES AND SHIP'S COMPONENTS

Hydrometer. VICKC-1256. Bearss number 1054.

Close-up of end of hydrometer (VICKC-1256) retaining original color.

HYDROMETER

Out of the depths of the Yazoo mud which once filled *Cairo* came a perfectly preserved glass hydrometer, recovered from the midships portion of the vessel. Discovery of the hydrometer was a minor miracle since this part of the vessel is one of the areas cut in half during the salvage operation. Furthermore, when the midships section came up, it was brought up to the surface sideways. The deck pointed straight up and down. The gun deck was upstream and the hold downstream. Coal was spilling out into the river.

When the barge carrying *Cairo* was brought to the bank, the Artifacts Committee went on board and from the mass of wood, mud and bent metal they retrieved combs, knives, shoes, bottles, tobacco, and numerous other items. On the second or third day of work someone found in the mud the hydrometer, unbroken. That it survived the salvage was miraculous; that it survived the feet of the workers was almost as miraculous. The red in the narrow glass tube was bright red and had not faded.

Consisting of a long glass tube, sealed, graduated, and made of clear glass, the hydrometer has a large bulb and smaller weighted bulb at end. Measuring 241 mm in length, the hydrometer has a diameter of 7.94 mm. Tube contains some type of measurement scale but is unreadable due to what appears to be rust on the outside of the glass.

Near top of tube is "200 FAHR" with "I" printed next to and above the "R." Red section between two bulbs. Smaller bulb contains tiny gray balls. Tube is weighted at one end; used to determine specific gravity. Instrument is complete and in good condition. Catalog number **VICKC-1256**. Bearss number 1054.

<h3 style="text-align:center">COMPASS</h3>

All that remains is the round brass case, small stem fragments (for hand to pivot on) and round glass top. Back of case is smaller in diameter than the front. The top rim angles out. Glass is loose, edges slightly chipped. Diameter (front of case) measures 44.5 mm; diameter (of glass): 42.9 mm; thickness (of case): 11.1 mm. The compass is incomplete and in poor condition. When compass was salvaged, a slender diamond-shaped hand was still attached; it is now gone. Catalog number **VICKC-1143**.

Compass. VICKC-1143.

<h3 style="text-align:center">SIGNAL BOARD</h3>

Wooden signal board with bell found in Pilot House is incomplete but in fair condition. Copper wires ran to the engine room to work the bells. Ferrous metal plate originally screwed to the top of board. Two bars on each side of plate form a groove for a long lever to slide up and down in one. One lever still has some of its wooden handle intact. Other handle is just a bare rod. Handles are at top of levers. At bottom of each lever is an eye. Copper wire twisted in the eye to fasten it. Copper wires are cut off below board. Board length measures 36" (914 mm) with a width of 11⅞" and a thickness of 1¾".

The bell was used to signal from pilot house (signal board) to engine room.

Heavy copper wires evidently ran from one place to the other. Both bell mechanism and signal board have short sections of wire still attached. Fairly large brass bell is mounted on a long, flat, heavy iron arm which is shaped like a question mark with the top end curled inward. Catalog number **VICKC-1493**.

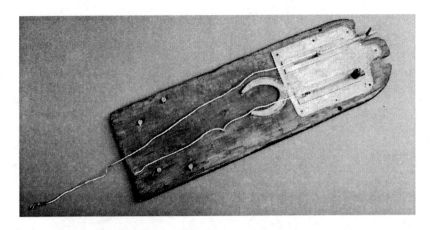

Signal board. VICKC-1493.

Only one bell was found with the signal board at time of recovery. A horseshoe was found tacked on the board, presumably for good luck.

BELL

This brass bell was used to signal from pilot house (signal board) to engine room. Heavy copper wires evidently ran from one place to

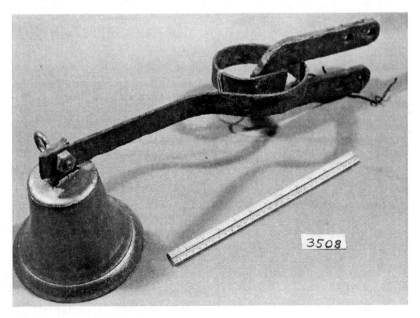

Brass bell from signal board. VICKC-1234. Bearss number 3508.

the other. Both bell mechanism and signal board have short sections of wire still attached. Fairly large bell is mounted on a long, flat, heavy iron arm which is shaped like a question mark with the top end curled in. The bell is incomplete but in good condition. Catalog number **VICKC-1234**. Bearss number 3508.

Map Paper

This linen-like map paper was found in the commissary storeroom in the same area that the drawing pen points were found. According to paper conservators at the Smithsonian Institution, the paper had not been used.

The roll of map paper was unrolled as carefully as possible, but the roll had

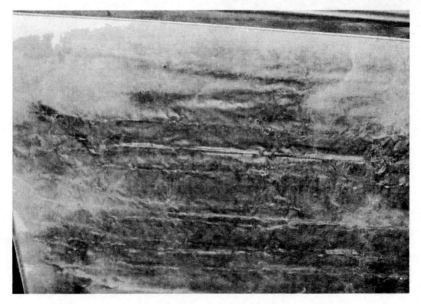

Map paper. VICKC-5430.

been in a section of the gunboat that fared badly in the salvage, and the paper roll had been crushed flat so that there were two sharp folds. The folds had broken through. The mud was washed away as gently as possible.

Once the map paper was thoroughly dry, it was placed in a large picture frame and the back sealed from the air. One small piece was left in the air. It disintegrated completely within a few weeks. Catalog number **VICKC-5430.**

STEAM GAUGE

Heavy round gauge made of brass. Back rim has three screw holes in it. Near top is the number "3647." At bottom is "Bourdon's/ Patent/Aug. 3, 1852." At bottom of the gauge is a ferrous metal threaded pipe fitting where pipe #1492 screws on. Face is covered by glass which is a modern replacement of the original. The scale on face goes from 0 to 220. Printed around the top of the opening at center

Steam gauge. VICKC-1491. Bearss number 3019.

is "Ashcroft's Steam Gauge Boston." Needle indicator is gone. The gauge is complete and in good condition. Catalog number **VICKC-1491**. Bearss number 3019.

STRONGBOX OR SAFE

The strongbox or safe was treated with a coat of red-orange rust preventive paint.

Close-up of steam gauge (VICKC-1491) showing patent date and information.

When the safe was discovered underwater by divers, the lock on the safe was broken. The safe has now been painted, cataloged and is presently in storage.

Strongbox or safe. VICKC-5175.

Front view of strongbox or safe.

The safe is described as an iron box with 30 × 43 cm door. Door swings on two 12-cm-long hinges. There is a 1.1-cm-diameter hole in edge of door where lock would have been attached. The door is dented and buckled slightly where someone pried the door open. The metal is in very good condition. Has been cleaned and treated with two coats of paint (red and black). Measuring: length: 50.8 cm; width: 37.7 cm; thickness: 30.2 cm. The safe is incomplete but in excellent condition. Catalog number **VICKC-5175.**

Anvil. VICKC-1963.

ANVIL

Ferrous metal. Black. Concave curves at base. Square waist hole is 25 mm wide. Edges are sharp. Imprinted on the body is "(illegible)/WRIGHT/PATENT." Measuring: length (of base) 184 mm; length (of face) 333 mm; length (of horn) 152 mm; height 270 mm. Anvil is complete but in fair condition. Catalog number **VICKC-1963**.

HATCH DOOR

Wooden door (complete), approximately 63 × 88 × 7 cm. Wood surface is scarred in numerous places, but overall condition is good. Assembled of three panels: 28 × 69 cm, 31 × 69 cm, 29 × 69 cm (all 7 cm thick). An iron handle, triangular, measuring 6 × 6 × 7.5 cm, is attached with a screw and 19 mm hexagonal nut. The iron fittings are oxidized but stable. Hatch is complete and in good condition. Catalog number **VICKC-4286**.

Hatch door. VICKC-4286.

DOOR

Narrow, rectangular, dark brown wooden door with two porcelain doorknobs. Portion of top missing. Door measures 160.1 × 58.6 cm. Worn butte stiles on top portion remain. One most worn has portion broken away. Top rail missing. Seven dowel holes in center stile.

Door—close up view. VICKC-2952.

Door. VICKC-2952.

Bottom door portion fairly intact. Some worn areas. Yellow green spots on one side along center stile. One panel and bottom rail. Doorknobs white. Dark brown staining. On one side is square metal. Lock plate (?) containing keyhole and secured with three protruding, oxidized, round, slotted head screws. Door is incomplete and in poor condition. Catalog number **VICKC-2952**.

FIREBOX FRAGMENT

Identified as "boiler fire door." Door is complete and in good condition measuring 38 × 35 cm. Two large iron plates. Base plate houses four threaded bolts and four dowels. Two bolts missing. Top plate houses nuts for bolts and tie bolt, a diamond-shaped hole, a round hole. The shape is not square. There is a protrusion on one side and welded trim around top piece. Bottom plate irregular also. Color is gray. Catalog number **VICKC-4421.**

Firebox fragment. VICKC-4421.

Crate fragment. VICKC-1232.

CRATE FRAGMENT

Bottom edge is complete. It has 3 nails in it and 2 other nail holes. Other 3 edges are broken. Some pieces still extant indicate this may have had a tongue and groove system. Wood is soft pine. Yellowish brown color. Has hand printed on it in script: "*hold gun Boat Cairo/ to be called for at Cairo Ex office.*" Used black ink or paint. Fragment measures 22⅜" in length by 5⅞" in width with a thickness of ⅝". Fragment is in good condition. Catalog number **VICKC-1232.**

THE "HOLLOW TREE" PUMPS

The bilge pump is made from hollow logs.

A hollow tree pump with small end planed for about 28 cm on one side with large portion of other side missing (length 17 cm). Center has large amounts of cracking and checking.

Large side lacks shape other than noticeable difference (length 10 cm) from size of center. Total measurement: length: 234.5 cm; hollow diameter: 13 cm. Large pieces missing from end. Pump incomplete but in fair condition. Catalog number **VICKC-4239.**

SHIP'S BELL

Bronze bell containing the following markings: cast by G W COFFIN & CO BUCKEYE BELL FOUNDRY CINCINNATI 1860 (marks ca. ¼ way down from top and encircle entire bell). Wider at

Cairo's bell. VICKC-2223.

flare. Ornamental near top, including flower pattern. Scratched. Numerous small chips at flare. Attached to black iron mount (pitted). Measuring: height 53 cm (73.5 cm including mounting bar); width 97 cm; circumference flare: 217.5 cm. Bell is complete and in good condition. Found in front of wheelhouse 30 September 1963. Catalog number **VICKC-2223.**

4

FURNITURE, FIXTURES AND LIGHTING

Furniture

Many furniture fragments were recovered. It is quite interesting to note what a hodge-podge of regular household furniture was used. Divers found parts of all sorts of chairs, including a rocking chair, a wicker chair and ladder-back chairs.

ROCKING CHAIR FRAGMENTS

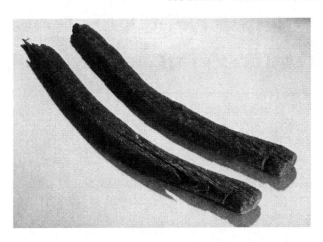

Rocking chair fragments (rockers). VICKC-2713.

Curved, slightly rounded wooden chair rockers (slats). One end "squared-off" contains rounded notch on bottom edge. Opposing end contains intentional split (6 cm in length) in center. One half is broken (large portion missing), other half contains a small hole in center. Long top edge contains rectangular hole (from where chair leg fit). Adjacent wood chips flaking away. Wood is shrunken, checked, dark in color. Measuring: length: 47.4 cm; width: 3.9 cm; thickness: 2.5 cm. Fragments in poor condition. Wood is shrunken and checked. Catalog number **VICKC-2713.**

FOLDING CHAIR FRAGMENT

Folding wooden legs from chair attached by a single bolt. One leg in better condition than the other. Protruding from a hole is threaded bolt end with square nut holding in place. Bolt on outer side of opposing leg topped with cap nut. Both legs have a bolt. Hole in more deteriorated leg extending through to opposite side. This leg worn. One end almost completely worn away. Much checking, some flaking, shallow digs throughout leg. Both legs coated with clear

Folding chair fragment. VICKC-2749.

lacquer (? PEG?), causing wood to be dark, glossy. Fragment is in poor condition. Measuring: length: 57 cm; thickness: 2.3 cm. Catalog number **VICKC-2749.**

These fragments possibly from camp or folding chair recovered from the pilot house. When this chair was first recovered, it had a wooden seat. On the bottom of the seat was stenciled, *CRAMS PATENT NO. 13479 Aug. 21, 1853 Boston.* The patent number was traced and plans for this chair were obtained through the Smithsonian. The chair went untreated from 1960 until 1964; consequently all that remains today are the folding legs. The chair was made of a type of soft pine.

BED FRAME

Metal bed frame. Twenty-four rope holders (or hooks). One round and curved brace (90.5 cm). Four long sharp-edged braces (92 to 93 cm each). Eight shorter-edged braces (23 to 51 cm each). Five rounded braces (74 cm each). Completely rusted throughout. Some rusted bolts holding the framework together. Measuring: length: 108 cm; width : 76 cm. Bed frame fragment is in good condition. Catalog number **VICKC-4290.**

Fixtures

The *Cairo* had bathroom facilities, although plans for the "City Class" gunboats did not show this bathroom.

Shower parts and a toilet bowl were found near the paddle wheel. Evidently water was supplied for these facilities by a trough from the wheel.

The shower head was brought up and was lying on the barge. One of the hired laborers, thinking the shower pipe was just an old pipe, tossed it overboard. The diver couldn't locate it again, and it was lost. Part of the shower pipe was recovered, but the pipe is not in the *Cairo* collection today. It may have been simply too fragile to preserve.

The toilet bowl is very fragile. It has not been sufficiently cleaned because no matter how gently we try to remove the corrosion, the commode cracks.

A faucet from the *Cairo* has also been preserved.

TOILET BOWL

Toilet. VICKC-870. Bearss number 2063.

Inside view of toilet (VICKC-870) showing matches.

Roughly funnel-shaped commode (cast iron?). Top slightly oval. Top edge has flat rim. "J.L. MOTT-IRON-WORKS/264–266/WATER-ST/N.Y." printed in raised letters on outside. Just under rim on inside, partially covering a hole, is a piece of rounded black metal, screwed on. Opposite, outside is pipe connection. Patches of rusty-yellow metal show through in places on inside. Brown substance covers most of inside,

Bottom view of toilet (VICKC-870) showing inscription.

has debris such as matchsticks stuck in it. Around middle on outside is band of heavily encrusted metal. Measuring: height: 222 mm; diameter (top): 430 mm; diameter (bottom): 114 mm.

Toilet is complete but is in poor condition with cracking throughout. Catalog number **VICKC-870**. Bearss number 2063.

FAUCET

Faucet. Mostly copper. Spout made in round "L" shape. Small leg of "L" turns down. Handle valve fits down into section of faucet that is at right angles to spout. Top of handle is ball-shaped. Rounded brass (?) handle grip is long, getting wider toward end. At back is short section of lead pipe. Uneven ridge near back edge. White encrustation inside. "...POWELL.../C..." barely legible printed on handle stem. Original catalog lists this as WM.POWELL & CO/CIN.O. Measuring: length: 140 mm; height: 122 mm; diameter (spout:) 23.8 mm. Faucet is complete and in good condition. Catalog number **VICKC-1421**.

FAUCET

Faucet. Mostly copper. Spout made in rounded L-shape. Small leg of "L" turns down. Handle valve fits down into section of faucet that is made at right angle to spout. Top of handle is ball-shaped. Rounded brass (?) handle grip: long, becoming wider toward end. At

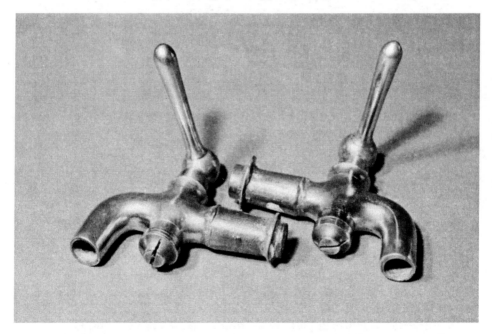

Faucet. VICKC-1421 and VICKC-1422.

back is short section of lead pipe. Uneven ridge near back edge. "W_POWELL & CO/CIN O" imprinted on handle stem. Tarnished. Measuring: length: 138 mm; height: 121 mm; diameter: 25.4 mm. Faucet is complete and in good condition. Catalog number **VICKC-1422.**

Lighting

LAMP GLOBE

Made of transparent glass. Much of soot still remains (globe has not been washed), giving a dark brown or black appearance to most of the glass. Round top (?). Has round opening, thick edges are turned out. Basal? Opening is larger; slightly chipped edges are greasy. Edges turned out. Top and bottom meet at an angle to form the sides. (It is difficult to tell which end is the top or bottom.) Measuring: diameter: 30.4 cm; base diameter: 11.7 cm; top diameter: 10.1 cm. Fragment is in good condition. Catalog number **VICKC-367.** Bearss number 2296.

Lamp globe. VICKC-367. Bearss number 2296. Top view.

Lamb globe. VICKC-367. Side view.

LAMP GLOBE

Clear, transparent glass lamp globe. This lamp is in a flying-saucer shape with an opening at the top and bottom. Edges of both openings are chipped. The top and bottom sides meet at a rounded angle. Some smoky, sooty areas remain. Measuring: height: 127 mm; top diameter: 87.3 mm; base diameter: 79.4 mm; width: 254 mm. Globe is in good condition. Catalog number **VICKC-388**.

LAMP GLOBE

Lamp globe made of clear, transparent glass. This globe is relatively tall, narrows toward the top and has round body. A band of tin around the base. Mold marks down each side. The top edge is rough. The edge of the base is chipped. One bubble in the side and a smaller one on bottom ridge. Measuring: height: 191 mm; top diameter: 69.9 mm; base diameter: 92.1 mm; width: 114 mm. Globe is in good condition. Catalog number **VICKC-386**.

Lamp globe. VICKC-388.

Lamp globe. VICKC-386.

LAMP BASE

Brass base and collar with two long screws holding brass plate under base in place. Cylindrical shaft held in place by the brass collar, which is welded to the shaft. Two holes not perfectly round are located at exact opposites of one another on the shaft. May have held another piece in place. Tin shaft is oxidized and brass is tarnished, showing signs of corrosion. Measuring: base diameter: 8.5 cm; screw length: 1.7 cm; shaft height: 7.5 cm. Lamp base is incomplete but in fair condition. Catalog number **VICKC-4399**.

Lamp base. VICKC-4399.

LAMP BASE

Round base with holes. Tube atop base. Two screws (probably to hold the brass cover in place). Tube is brass and contains organic debris, which consists of bits of white claylike substance. Most of this artifact is covered with the same white substance. Measuring: height: 13 cm; round base diameter: 5 cm; base height: 3 cm. Holes in Base: diameter: 3 mm. Tube Height: 9.5 cm; tube diameter: 2 cm. Base is incomplete and in poor condition. Catalog number **VICKC-4366**.

Lamp base. VICKC-4366.

LAMP BASE

Oil lamp top. Brass lamp pipe or tube. Nipple and nut are one piece, hanging loose on shaft. The cap, with 25 holes is attached to the shaft. It is also made of brass. The cap has billowing rounds. The first one is flat, 1 cm from the second. The third follows immediately, then the last that accommodates the holes. The next is tapered and sits on the shaft, separated by, perhaps, a washer. The nipple is stripped and gouged at the end. Tarnish throughout. Base is complete and in good condition. Measuring: length: 13 cm; width: 6 cm; cap diameter: 17 cm. Catalog number **VICKC-4367**.

Lamp base—VICKC-4367.

CANDLE FRAGMENTS

Pieces of white candles, made of spermaceti according to the original catalog account. Wick still extant, will burn. Fragments are

Candle fragments. VICKC-1225. Bearss number 1048.

badly eroded with uneven surfaces. Dirt clings to surface making them look brown. Measuring: length: 1⅛" (47.6 mm)—5¼" (133 mm); diameter: ⁵⁄₁₆" (7.94 mm)—⅝" (15.9 mm). In poor condition. Catalog number **VICKC-1225**. Bearss number 1048.

SIGNAL LANTERN

Made of tinned iron. Rectangular box shape. Top is made in an arch shape; over another piece also is an arch shape, mounted the opposite way. Mounted on the top is a brass wire loop handle and a brass catch to hold front of lantern when open. The front is made of two pieces. One is a square, hinged (at top) door with a small brass handle; the other is the front part of lantern. It has a round opening at the center. Just below this is a brass catch to fasten the door shut. Front of lantern was hinged on the side. Back of lantern has 3 brass wire loops. Inside lantern is a round reflector mounted on the back.

Signal lantern. VICKC-1230.

One square piece of tin, loose, has a large opening at the center. Piece of tin at bottom holds the lamp parts. Two small wick holders (?) extend out an opening at the top. On the front is a wire ring in a bracket. "M. M. RUCK/MAKR/(symbol)/54 VINE ST/ST.LOUIS." printed on front. Measuring: height with handle: 10". Lantern is complete and in good condition. Catalog number **VICKC-1230.**

WICK TRIMMER

Shaped somewhat like a pair of scissors. Made of 2 pieces of ferrous metal which cross at the center and pivot. Held by a small rivet. One of the pieces comes to a sharp point at one end. The other has a wide flat "pelican bill" shaped section at the end. This section has a vertical curved edge on it made of brass. The beginning of the handle is flat, then it curves upward. Both oval finger holes badly rusted away. Measuring: length: 5¹³⁄₁₆" (148 mm); maximum width: 1" (25.4 mm). Trimmer is in fair condition with some oxidation and pitting. Catalog number **VICKC-1222.**

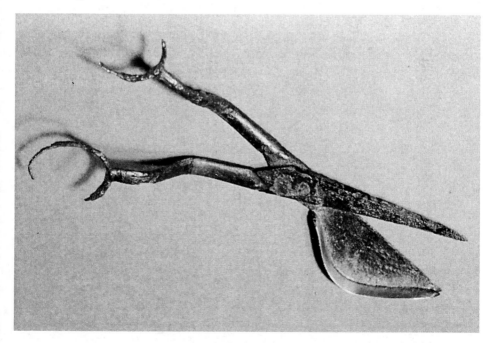

Wick trimmer. VICKC-1222.

5

COOKWARE AND EATING UTENSILS

ICE CHEST

This double ice chest was never soaked in polyethylene glycol. It was painted twice with thin coats of about 20-percent solution of polyethylene glycol. Faint traces of powdering can be seen if you look closely at the ice chest. It looks like a thin coat of dust.

The ice chest is a wooden chest with attached lid. Lid has latch fastened to front. Top of lid has board attached to left side with 12 screws. No board remains attached to right side of lid. Chest is double lined with smaller lid. This lid has broken portion of latch still evident. Rounded wooden blocks from which iron handles are

Ice chest. VICKC-3605.

"Southern Belle" cooking range. VICKC-5525.

attached protrude from either side. Dovetailing along each corner. Wood inside of top lid is darker in color than wood inside of chest. Wood along front of chest is colored and streaked. The chest is complete and in good condition. Measuring: inner length: 40.5 cm; inner width: 66.2 cm; outer length: 55.0 cm; outer width: 69.3 cm. Catalog number **VICKC-3605**.

"SOUTHERN BELLE" COOKING RANGE

The cooking range from the USS *Cairo*, which was ironically called a "Southern Belle," was bent during the salvage. Because of its weight, it was left on the barge for a long time. Finally, when the boilers were brought in to the park, the stove was also brought in. Unfortunately by this time the stove had rusted badly after more than a year's exposure to the elements. Catalog number **VICKC-5525**.

There are stove eyes, miscellaneous doors, and broken pieces. One diver commented to Margie Bearss that in two different places

"Southern Belle" cooking range (VICKC-5525). Close view of stove plate.

in the officers' quarters there were small pot bellied stoves. A few of the parts fit these smaller stoves.

ROLLING PIN

Very dark wood heavily impregnated with polyethylene glycol (PEG). Some PEG deposited on one side making it look waxy. Orig-

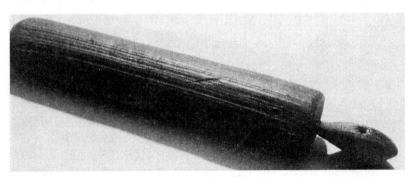

Rolling pin. VICKC-1198.

inally round, but now somewhat flattened. One handle broken off. Other is rounded. One side is flattened, has wax on it. Horizontal hole through handle. It is held by a metal pin onto rolling pin. Will turn. Measuring: length 14⅜". Rolling pin is complete and in fair condition. Catalog number **VICKC-1198**.

PIE PAN

Pie pan. VICKC-958.

Made of tinned iron. Shallow. Bottom is flat. Sides are short, slanted outward. Top edge is bent back underneath. Utensil scratch marks on inside bottom. Measuring: height: 1¼" (31.8 mm); diameter across bottom: 6¹¹⁄₁₆" (170 mm); diameter across top: 8⁹⁄₁₆" (217 mm). The pie pan is in fair condition with several large holes on the bottom where it has rusted out. Other rusty areas and scratches on the bottom. Small break along the edge. Tin is generally gray. Slightly bent along top edge and across the bottom. Catalog number **VICKC-958**.

COFFEEPOT

Tall cylindrical container made of tinned iron. A vertical seam down one side. The top is slightly convex and is joined to the main part with a seam around the top. The pour spout is soldered on at the center of the top. It is cylindrical with a seam down one side. Two handles. A wire carrying handle at the top is attached at each side by being bent back through a bracket. On each side of the top a tin bracket with a hole in it is soldered on. The other handle is a pouring handle. Height, 286.0 mm; bottom diameter, 106.0 mm; spout diameter, 28.6 mm. Coffeepot is incomplete, but in good condition. Catalog number **VICKC-611.** Bearss number 2016.

Coffeepot. VICKC-611. Bearss number 2016.

COFFEEPOT

Made of tinned iron. Truncated cone shape. Top smaller in diameter than the base. Seam down both sides has thick finished edge on outside, black sealing substance on inside. Bottom is flat, has edge turned up over bottom edge of sides. Pouring handle broken off. Only the two rivets which held the handle's top and one which held the bottom, a fragment of handle, and the black sealer are still intact on the back. A bracket for lifting handle is riveted to each side of the top. Broken pieces of a wire handle are still over it, making a rounded edge. On the front a rounded "V" shaped pouring spout is riveted on and has black sealer. The pot has a section of holes in a "V" shape behind the

Coffeepot. VICKC-1205. Bearss number 2633.

spout. Measuring: height: 9⅟₁₆" (230 mm); diameter of base: 7⅝" (194 mm); diameter of top: 5½" (140 mm). Coffeepot is incomplete but in fair condition. Catalog number **VICKC-1205**, Bearss number 2633.

MESS CHESTS AND THEIR CONTENTS

Two complete mess chests were brought up intact with contents just as they were placed after breakfast on December 12, 1862.

Each chest contained 13 mess plates, 13 spoons, 13 cups, a dish pan (rectangular and deep), a brush, a sponge, a jug (one had traces of molasses), a strainer, a coffee container, and several glass bottles of Navy-issue mustard and pepper.

The mess plates and cups are of tinned iron—which is a thin coat of tin over iron. These are all in varying conditions. Some are like new. Some are rusted fragments. The most interesting are those personalized by the sailors themselves. Many scratched their initials neatly and legibly. Some, unable to write, scratched designs or marks on their cups, spoons, and plates. These present a problem. Most of the

Mess chest with contents. VICKC-1182.

time, the men scratched deeply, cutting through the thin layer of tin. The iron beneath the tin rusted easily and the rust is eating into these scratched names and marks in a way that is almost impossible to stop.

When the marks were shallow and not through the tin, rust has not progressed. Sam W. Chandler's mess plate, scratched lightly on the bottom, is one of the best preserved.

One mess chest is a very large rectangular wooden box. Measuring: length: 44"; width: 20⅜"; height: 17¾". Original lid is missing. Ferrous metal staple-like loop mounted on the front. Vertical hasp held on this by the padlock. Padlock # 1184 still locked on the loop. Hasp is loose. Ends and sides joined with dovetailed joints nailed in place. One bottom side edge has a long strip of wood attached, making a leg. Each end has a handle held on with 4 heavy screws. Next to the chest the handle is flat. The top is curved horizontally. Hole through the middle. Chest is incomplete but in good condition. Catalog number **VICKC-1182**.

Mess plate (upside down showing star). VICKC-606.

Another example of a mess plate with initials still visible on plate bottom.

MESS PLATE

Mess plate made of tinned iron. The bottom is flat and the sides slope outward. The top edge is rounded and is turned down around a concealed wire rim. Three vertical side seams. Thick ridge at seam on the outside. Also a seam where bottom and sides meet. Scratched deeply into the tin on the bottom is a crude 5-pointed star. Scratched in very lightly is the name "J.A. Lee." These letters are very faint now. Utensil marks on bottom very numerous; some of tin finish is gone. Measuring: height: 58.7 mm; bottom diameter: 159. 0 mm; top diameter: 208.0 mm. Catalog number **VICKC-606.**

SERVING PITCHER

Serving pitcher. VICKC-462.

Heavy copper pitcher, round. Vertical seam down the back underneath the handle. Handle is attached by two rivets at top and halfway down the side. Handle has a reinforcing piece underneath. Lip of pitcher extends half of the way around the top opening. The sides are plain and straight, tapering toward the top. The bottom is plain and flat. All edges and seams are finished by turning a narrow edge. Inside is black. Outside finish in good condition. Measuring: height 254.0 mm; diameter: 170.0 mm; width: 241.0 mm. Pitcher is complete and in good condition. Catalog number **VICKC-462.**

IRONSTONE PLATE

White ironstone plate. Crazed. Many of the craze lines have taken on a darker color. Top: center section has definite dish shape (may be a soup plate). Sides of center section quite rounded. Wide rim slopes gradually outward. Bottom: center section is flat. Has lettering stamped in plate, barely legible: "T? &—BOO?/WARRANTY?" (may be inaccurate). Ridge around edge of center section. Convex sides. Rim slopes gradually upward. Measuring: height: 1½" (3.810 cm); top diameter: 9¹¹⁄₁₆" (24.606 cm); base diameter: 5¹⁄₁₆" (12.859 cm). Condition good. Not chipped or broken. Light brown stain on one part of front. Catalog number **VICKC-316.**

Two overall views of an officer's place setting. Ironstone plate VICKC-316 is at the center of the setting.

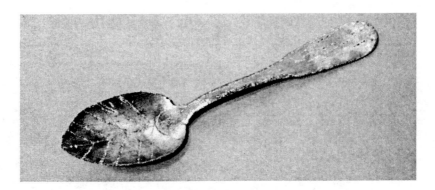

Spoon with leaf design. VICKC-702.

SPOON WITH LEAF DESIGN

Large tablespoon made of tinned iron. Bowl and handle are riveted together. The bowl is shallow and comes to a point at the end. Both edges of the throat are turned down slightly. Throat gets wider where handle begins. The handle is wide and flat with a rounded end. Manufacturer's mark on throat barely legible "Pat....-8—." The front of the bowl has a design scratched in it like the veins of a leaf. Four vertical scratch marks on handle. Color rather dark. Edges of bowl rusted, rough. Measuring: length 184.0 mm; maximum width of bowl: 41.3 mm. Spoon is complete and in fair condition. Catalog number **VICKC-702.** Bearss number 1829.

SPOON

Large tablespoon made of tinned iron. Bowl and handle are riveted together. Bowl is shallow and comes to a point at the end. Sides

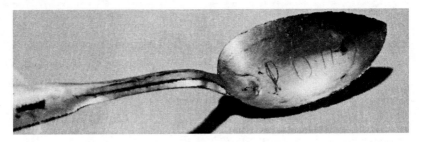

Spoon showing initials "POH."

of throat have a small slanted edge. Throat gets wider where handle begins. Handle is wide and slightly turned up. Scratched on end of handle is "HHH" (similar to pattern). Initials "POH" scratched in bowl. (Recovered from quartermaster's storeroom; likely belonged to crewman Peter Ole Hill.) Edges of bowl rough, notches around handle edge. Shiny finish gone along top edges of throat in two spots on handle. Measuring: length 187.0 mm, maximum width of bowl: 41.3 mm. Spoon is complete and in fair condition. Catalog number **VICKC-1928.**

SPONGES

About a half dozen sponges (natural) ranging from 6 to 12 inches across were recovered during the raising. Sponges were stored in large-mouthed gallon jars obtained from the kitchen of the Catholic school once they were brought up out of the river.

SPONGE

Small piece of a natural sponge. Flat. Outside is brown. Inside along broken edge looks somewhat darker. Shape roughly round. Still

Sponges. VICKC-614 and VICKC-615.

rather spongy. Feels fuzzy. Measuring: diameter: 54.0 mm; thickness: 14.3 mm. Sponge is complete and in good condition. Catalog number **VICKC-614**.

SPONGE

Small natural sponge. Dark brown. Irregular shape. Still feels spongy. Fine fibers in the sponge. One area has some grease on it, making it slightly darker. Measuring: approximate length: 95.3 mm; maximum width: 57.2 mm. Sponge is complete and in good condition. Catalog number **VICKC-615**.

BAKING PAN

Long shallow rectangular baking pan. Tinned iron. Painted black. Sides slope gently outward. Top edge turned down over wire rim. Handles on each opposite short side. Bracket held on by 2 rivets. Handle turns in this. At each corner is fold on outside. Rusted through with numerous medium-size holes on one side and bottom where pan is bent. Other small rust holes. Rust encrustation inside. Measuring: length: 511 mm; height: 57.2 mm; width: 310 mm. Pan is complete

Baking pan. VICKC-871.

and in fair condition. This item was found inside of the cooking range (VICKC-5525) upon its recovery. Catalog number **VICKC-871.**

Copper Tea Kettle

Large copper teakettle. Round, squat shape. Bottom piece round. It rests on a base which is smaller in diameter than the sides. Long spout is curved. Scallop at the mouth. Seam down both sides of main part. Top is convex. Round opening in center for lid. Lid is convex with a brass knob on top. Handle attached to kettle's handle brackets with a brass washer and rivet. Handle brackets attached to kettle with 2 brass rivets. Handle is arched. Measuring: height with handle: 12" (305 mm); height without handle: 9" (229 mm) including lid; maximum width with spout: 13¼" (337 mm); diameter of base: 6½" (165 mm). Tea kettle is complete and in good condition. Catalog number **VICKC-1487.** Bearss number 2014.

Copper tea kettle. VICKC-1487. Bearss number 2014.

Measuring cups. VICKC-596, VICKC-457, and VICKC-447.

MEASURING CUPS

Round tin cups, no handles. On each, bottom is convex. The sides taper inward toward the top. Seam down one side. Also a seam where sides meet bottom. The top edge is turned out and down over a metal ring. The top is open. Measuring cups in fair to good condition. Catalog numbers **VICKC-596, VICKC-457,** and **VICKC-447.**

WINE GLASS FRAGMENT

Part of the foot of a stemmed wine goblet or similar glass. Glass is transparent. The bottom side is concave. The glass gets thinner toward the edge. Round piece of thick glass where stem began. Measuring: length: 55.6 mm; width: 41.3 mm; thickness: 12.7 mm. Fragment is in good condition. Catalog number **VICKC-444.**

Wine glass fragment. VICKC-444.

Slanted type tin mess cup. VICKC-1188.

MESS CUP

Slant type. Made of tinned iron. Sides made of one piece of tin with a seam down one side. Seam has a thick finished edge. Bottom edge turned up over bottom edge of sides. Top has a concealed wire rim with the tin bent down over it making a rounded edge. Arched handle is attached in front of side seam. Handle is wider at the top. The edges are turned inside. At the top there is a partially concealed wire going out from each edge and looped over the top rim to attach the handle top. Also a black solder-like sealing material along handle top. Bottom of handle is riveted on. Measuring: top diameter: 4⅛"; base diameter: 4⅝"; height: 3¹⁵⁄₁₆". Catalog number **VICKC-1188**.

MESS CUP

"Two ring" type. More accurately described as one raised ridge or ring and a groove. Made of tinned iron. Sides are straight, made of one piece of tin with a seam down one side. Seam has a thick

Two-ring type tin mess cup. VICKC-1189.

finished edge. Top has a concealed wire rim with the tin bent down
over it making a rounded edge. Unusual handle. Shaped roughly like
a question mark. Edges turned inside. Heavy rust makes rivets difficult
to see. At least one rivet holds top of handle on. One rivet also at
bottom. Handle attached on the side seam. Bottom gone. Personal
scratch marks "CA." Measuring: top diameter: 4¼"; height: 4⁹⁄₁₆". Catalog number **VICKC-1189.**

BARREL

Barrel with a circumference around center of 95.9 cm and 86.4
cm circumference around each end. It is 42 cm tall with a 3.5-cm
diameter hole in one of the staves through which the contents can
be viewed. Contents appear to be nutmeg mixed with sand and debris.
Staves are untreated wood, ranging in width from 3 cm to 5.2 cm.
Each is 5 mm thick. Seventeen total staves make up the body of the

Barrel still containing original contents thought to be nutmeg. VICKC-5176.

Barrel lid half. VICKC-4183.

barrel. Four iron bands, two at ends, still attached. Center bands have fallen off but are still present. Iron is very oxidized and deteriorated. Barrel is sealed (lid is still attached). Barrel is complete and in poor condition. Catalog number **VICKC-5176.**

BARREL LID HALF

Semicircular wood segment, Long base is 34 cm; from top of arc to base is 18.5 cm; 1 cm thick. Light wood, probably pine; black stenciling still visible on one side. "INSP," "CAIRO" only letters still legible. Catalog number **VICKC-4183.** Measuring: long Base: 34 cm, L (from top of arc to base) 18.5 cm. Barrel lid half is in good condition.

6

BOTTLES

Soda pop bottles. VICKC-1214, VICKC-87 and VICKC-88.

SODA POP BOTTLES

Soda pop bottles with no remaining contents. Heavy blue-green transparent glass. Body of each is cylindrical and tapers as the shoulders curve gently inward in conical fashion. Mold mark down each side. Heavy, thick, bulbous collar formed at neck terminus by a separate piece of glass. Neck has twist lines in the glass. Each bottle has a few bubbles in the glass. Base has a dished center. Glass has a grainy texture and many fine scratches with a worn look to surface. Around body is printed in large, slightly raised capital letters: "J. H. KUMP"; below this is printed in a different script, "MEMPHIS/TENN." Measuring: Height: 7⅝" (194 mm); diameter of base: 2⅝" (66.7 mm); diameter of neck (inside) ¹³⁄₁₆" (20.6 mm); diameter of neck (outside) 1³⁄₁₆" (30.2 mm). Bottles in good condition, some chips. Catalog numbers **VICKC-1214, VICKC-87 and VICKC-88.**

Lea & Perrins Worcestershire Sauce bottle. VICKC-1215. Bearss number 2787.

WORCESTERSHIRE SAUCE BOTTLE

Made of light green transparent glass, now very cloudy. No contents. Cylindrical body. Long cylindrical neck. Collar has a rounded band on top, flat slant section and is lettered horizontally to read "WORCESTERSHIRE SAUCE." Lettered vertically on one side is "LEA & PERRINS." Base has a flat edge and a dished depression bearing in raised letters "Co A C B." Measuring: height: 7" (178 mm); diameter of base: 2" (50.8 mm); diameter of neck (inside) $^{11}/_{16}$" (17.5 mm); diameter of neck (outside) 1" (25.4 mm). Bottle in good condition. Found by naval intelligence men. Catalog number **VICKC-1215.** Bearss number 2787.

MUSTARD AND PEPPER CONDIMENT BOTTLES

Many of these types of bottles were recovered during the salvage, leading one to believe that meals aboard *Cairo* were very bland. The pepper bottles have retained their distinct pepper scent after having remained in the depths of the Yazoo River for over 100 years.

MUSTARD BOTTLE

Octagonal, light aqua color. Transparent glass with streaks of hazy white. A few tiny bubbles. Eight facets are approximately 1.905 cm wide and end in slight scallops at the neck where they form narrow shoulders. Neck is cylindrical. Thin lip is folded inside forming narrow ridge. Slightly irregular on one facet is printed "U.S. NAVY" in raised letters; on the side opposite is printed "MUSTARD." Faint mold mark evident across the base. Has wide, flat edge and slightly depressed circular center. Measuring: height: 5⅜" (13.653 cm). Traces of dry mustard retained along the inner lip area of the bottle. Catalog number **VICKC-64**.

Mustard bottle. VICKC-64.

PEPPER CONDIMENT BOTTLE

Octagonal shaped. Transparent aqua-colored glass. Hazy patches. There are many tiny bubbles within the glass. Each of the 8 facets is

Pepper bottle. VICKC-4102.

approximately 1.905 cm wide, tapering inward at the neck and ending in an irregular line. "U.S. NAVY" printed on one facet in raised letters. "PEPPER" printed on opposite facet. Neck is cylindrical. Lip folded inside forming a very irregular ridge. Top not level. Base has flat edge, recessed circular center. Very faint mold mark. Measuring:

Pepper from condiment bottle.

height: 5⁷⁄₁₆" (13.811 cm); diameter of base: 1¹³⁄₁₆" (4.604 cm); diameter
of neck (inside) 1¹⁄₁₆" (2.699 cm); diameter of neck (outside) 1⁵⁄₁₆" (3.334
cm). Bottle in good condition. Catalog number **VICKC-4102.**

PEPPER FROM CONDIMENT BOTTLE

These are 31.9 grams of black pepper. Evenly ground black
pepper. Clotted together in clumps ranging in diameter from 0.1 mm
to 19 mm. Coarse ground. Each grain "sand size" (0.05 mm). Char-
coal black in color. In excellent condition.

CATHEDRAL BOTTLE

Transparent aqua-colored glass. The body bears six inset gothic
panels or windows, two opposing pairs of which have an extra ridge
of glass forming a frame around the circumference. Above each panel
on the shoulders are smaller 5-sided windows with a central depressed
3-lobed element. A single floral motif tops each small window on the
shoulders. The neck terminates in a relatively wide, rounded, tooled
collar with a slightly beveled rim at the base. Base has a flat edge that
slants toward center. Concave center. Slightly off-centered. Mold mark.
Flaw in neck. 14.3 mm bubble in one panel. Measuring: height: 221

Cathedral bottle. VICKC-1886.

mm; diameter (of base) 54.0 mm; diameter (of neck, outside) 30.2 mm. Originally contained pepper sauce, now retains no contents. Bottle is in complete and good condition. Catalog number **VICKC-1886**.

PEPPER SAUCE

According to records from the raising, a bottle of pepper sauce was recovered. It is thought that a sailor had taken a champagne bottle and put vinegar and small hot peppers into it. The bottle was sealed with a cork stopper. After a few weeks, the cork started to shrink and crack. The smell of pepper sauce came out clear and strong.

DR. FORSHA'S ALTERATIVE BALM BOTTLE

Medicine bottle. Aqua glass, transparent. Roughly rectangular. Front, back have recessed center panel, slanted side panel on each side. Printed vertically on front center panel (to be read horizontally) in raised letters: "DR. FORSHA'S ALTERATIVE BALM." "DR. FORSHA'S" printed on back. Narrow side panel each end. Shoulder rounded on ends, flat on sides. Neck is long and cylindrical. Collar

Dr. Forsha's Alterative Balm bottle—First bottle brought to the surface by diver Ken Parks. VICKC-1394. Bearss number 2933.

E. R. Squibb medicine bottle still containing original contents. VICKC-12. Bearss number 2307.

rounded at top, slanted band below, rounded lip. Base has wide flat edges on ends, narrow on sides. Base very thick at middle. Unusual mold mark. Catalog number **VICKC-34**. Bearss number 2933. Measuring: height: 168 mm; length: 79.4 mm (base); width: 41.3 mm (base). Bottle in complete and good condition. According to *Cairo* diver Ken Parks, this was the first bottle that was brought to the surface. Bearss number 2933.

MEDICINE BOTTLE

Dark green transparent glass. Upper portion of glass stopper rounded. A few bubbles in glass. Cylindrical body and neck. Rounded shoulders. "E.R. SQUIBB" printed in raised letters on the shoulder.

Separate piece of glass at end of neck forms wide, asymmetrical collar. Concave base with smooth bump at center. Still retaining its original contents of distilled water. Measuring: height 6¼" (15.875 cm) without stopper; diameter of base 2⁹⁄₁₅" (6.509 cm); diameter of neck (outside) 1" (2.540 cm). In complete and good condition. Catalog number **VICKC-12**. Bearss numbers 2037.

DECANTER

Fancy flask of blue-green transparent glass. Basically pear shaped; two long flat sides, two rounded sides, iridescent. Molded

Decanter. VICKC-86.

with a pattern of scroll lines in the glass. A few bubbles. Neck is roughly cylindrical. Collar is uneven with a crude, flat lip. Oval-shaped base slants inward toward circular dished center. Uneven mold mark. No original contents remaining. Measuring: height 18.415 cm; base diameter 4.445 cm. In complete and good condition. Catalog number **VICKC-86.**

7

CLOTHING AND FABRIC

Cloth Items

Scraps of cloth of various types were found all over the vessel. The cotton of the shirts didn't last, nor did the underwear. Buttons from both were found. Fragments of the wool of winter uniforms were found in numerous places on the vessel. Only in two cases were the buttons attached to the material. One of these large fragments is on display in the museum. In several instances machine stitching showed. The machine stitches were all of a uniform length.

There was one large knitted object which seemed to be a shawl. It had a strange color—a sort of pink and brown. It looked as if it had originally been red and brown. One piece of tweed (dark green with turquoise flecks) held up well. The cloth was washed carefully in tepid water with Ivory Snow detergent. It was not scrubbed or wrung as wringing would have snapped the fragile threads. There were a number of pea jackets which disintegrated almost immediately leaving only 5 black hard rubber buttons.

There were traces of burlap, but none was saved.

About a hundred neckerchiefs were brought up. Three were washed as the Smithsonian advised. These are intact. The others were not washed carefully or gently enough. They range in condition from shreds to those that split into several pieces.

The red flannel is from bags that held the black powder. This cloth loses its color when exposed to light—most of it was faded when it was brought in.

All the cloth brought in, no matter how small the fragment, was treated the same way, except for the majority of the neckerchiefs, which were put into a big tank and a hose turned on them. When the worker saw the result of the strong stream of water, he left the neckerchiefs for Margie Bearss to treat with the rest of the cloth. The same method of drying was used that was used for the paper. It was during the drying period that the cloth would disintegrate. After working a bit with a few fragments (a sort of trial-and-error method) Margie discovered a way to dry the material slowly enough to save it. She spread three heavy towels. On them she put a layer of the freshly washed (but not squeezed or wrung) cloth from Cairo. (Husband Ed didn't have any towels for a while because Margie was using their own supply of towels from home to dry out the neckerchiefs). Next she put another layer of towels, then a layer of cloth, until the stack was several inches tall.

Margie rolled the towels into a thick, compact roll. Next she sprinkled the entire outside of the roll with water from a clothes sprinkler. This allowed drying from the inside of the roll. Several times over a period of about two months she dampened the outside towels. When the entire stack was absolutely dry (several months later) the cloth was removed. It was placed in glass jars away from the air. One or two crystals of moth nuggets (which protects from mildew as well as from insects) were placed in each jar. The tops were screwed on tightly to prevent air from entering. Inside one or two jars, a few drops of moisture collected. The tops were removed and the cloth wrapped in dry towels for several days. The cloth was then replaced in the jars.

Some very interesting items were found attached to cloth fragments. One fragment of a uniform shirt had a pocket which contained a drawing pen point and a white underwear button. A rating badge (sleeve) was found, but was never brought into the workshop. Also, an almost-complete pair of overalls was found in the powder room. They were made of Navy blue cloth, wide wale like corduroy. The threads had deteriorated, but a large number of pieces of the garment are intact—the straps and the overall buckles are also there.

One tiny fragment of each type of material was sealed in plastic so the colors would not fade.

NECKERCHIEF

Made of black silk. Folded. Was originally, when salvaged, still tied. Same type material as **VICKC-1819**, but a little larger in size. Numerous mud stains. Many places where threads are loose and weak. Along the edge is a border consisting of 5 heavier threads. Fine

Neckerchief. VICKC-1817.

Neckerchief folded in a triangle. VICKC-1819. Bearss number 4233.

black powder results from handling. Fragile. Measuring: folded rectangular: 152 mm × 210 mm (when opened). Neckerchief complete and in fair condition. This piece received conservation treatment at Harpers Ferry Center. Catalog number **VICKC-1817**.

NECKERCHIEF

Made of black silk. Folded in a triangle. Same type of material as **VICKC-1817**, but smaller. Identified by Margie Bearss as a neckerchief because it was, when salvaged, still tied in a knot. Numerous stains. Many places where threads are loose and weak. Along the edge is a border consisting of 5 heavier threads. Fine black powder results from handling. Fragile. Measuring: folded rectangular: 216 mm × 159 mm. Neckerchief complete and in fair condition. This piece received conservation treatment at Harpers Ferry Center. Catalog number **VICKC-1819**. Bearss number 4233.

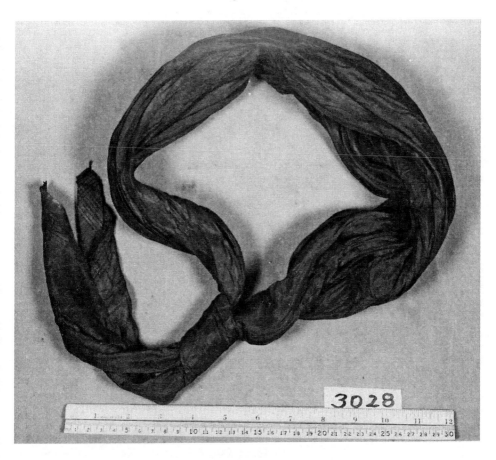

Neckerchief still knotted from last time worn by *Cairo* sailor.
VICKC-1851. Bearss number 3028.

NECKERCHIEF

Made of black silk. Still tied in knot as it was worn. Border along
edge made of parallel lines of heavier thread. Described in *American
Military Equipage Vol. III* as "a square-shaped piece of silk, probably
three feet on a side, worn underneath the collar of the Frock." Very
light mud stains in a very few places. Quite bunched up, wrinkled,
where it fit under collar. Retains original shape. Material in excellent
condition. Measuring: length: 584 mm; thickness (of knot): 23.8 mm.
Neckerchief complete and in fair condition. Catalog number **VICKC-
1851**. Bearss number 3028.

Hatband with "CAIRO" printed in gold lettering. VICKC-1818.
Bearss number 3029.

HATBAND

"CAIRO" is printed in gold lettering on a thin black silk ribbon. Top and bottom edges are complete. Row of stitching holes along
the edge beneath lettering. Both ends are frayed. Several small holes
in ribbon. Some mud stains. Gold letters have faded. Gold color has
come off in places. Measuring: width: 36.5 mm; length: 422 mm.
Hatband is complete and in fair condition. This piece received
conservation treatment at Harpers Ferry Center. Catalog number
VICKC-1818. Bearss number 3029.

VEST

Made of dark blue or black wool. Rounded edge on one side.
Four buttonholes near this edge. Row of stitch holes along bottom

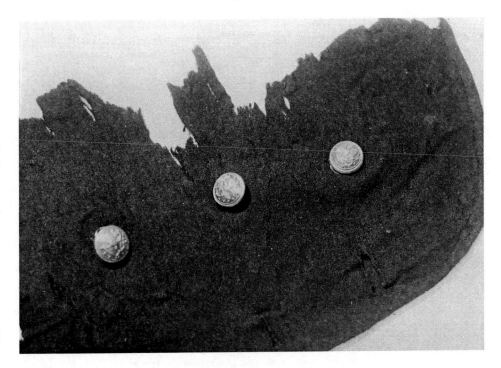

Vest. VICKC-1820.

rounded edge. Sewn to a backing to stabilize (at Harpers Ferry Center). Other edge of vest is torn, uneven. Row of (3) buttons still attached (2) by their original brass loops. Buttons are the Sanders Type—U.S. Navy Button. Button is backmarked "SCOVILL MFG. CO. WATERBURY." Front has in relief an eagle quartering to the left. Upper fluke behind left wing. Measuring: length (of vest) 378 mm; width: 222 mm; diameter (of button) 19.1 mm. Vest is incomplete and in poor condition. This piece received conservation treatment at Harpers Ferry Center. Catalog number **VICKC-1820.** Bearss number 3029.

COAT SLEEVE

Made of heavy, light blue wool. Flat, no longer stitched together. Has faded to a dull, brownish color. Hidden areas are a darker blue. One edge is turned. Cuff made of an added piece of material, edges turned under. Was originally machine stitched, according to Margie

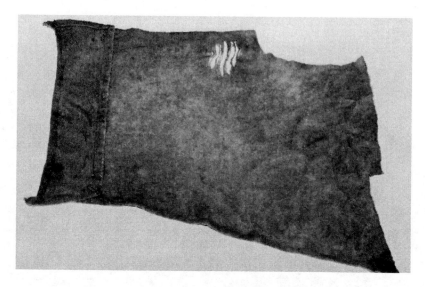

Coat sleeve. VICKC-1821.

Bearss. Small Buttonhole at bottom cuff edge. Hole in fabric. Not complete. Fragment is in fair condition. Measuring: length: 432 mm; width: 279 mm. This piece received conservation treatment at Harpers Ferry Center. Catalog number **VICKC-1821.**

CLOTH FRAGMENT

Small piece of dark brown woven cloth, possibly flannel. Cloth is folded and bunched. The edges are frayed. There appear to be holes

throughout. Measuring: length: 11 cm; width. 6.8 cm (irregularly shaped). Fragment is in poor condition. Catalog number **VICKC-3881.**

CLOTH FRAGMENT

Black fragment of what appears to be made of wool with some dirt and debris still adhering. A tear along

Cloth fragment. VICKC-4133.

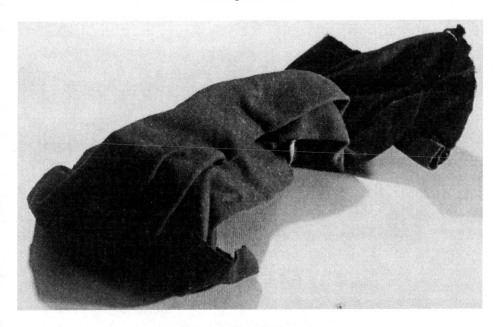

Cloth fragment. VICKC-4842.

one side measuring 3.2 cm and a 2 mm hole. Rectangular in shape, three sides appear to have been cut, and there is stitching along one side. Measuring: 14.6 cm × 7.1 cm. Fragment is in excellent condition. Catalog number **VICKC-4133.**

CLOTH FRAGMENT

Thick (approximately 0.2 cm) navy blue wool; Margie Bearss describes as "like pea coat material." Measuring: (approximate) length: 33 cm; Width: 34 cm. Fragment in good condition. Catalog number **VICKC-4842.**

Sewing Notions

SEWING NEEDLE

Large needle made of ferrous metal. At the top the needle has 2 sides. The main part has 3 flat sides. These sides taper gradually to form a sharp point. Rectangular eye. Imprinted on one side is

Sewing needle (VICKC-481) and Thread (VICKC-1086).

"R SCHOFIELD." Measuring: length: 73.0 mm; width: 3.18 mm. Needle is complete and in good condition. Catalog number **VICKC-481.**

THREAD

Several of the braids were found originally but this is the only one partially intact. Contains about (100) separate threads. One end is a neat braid. The other end is a tangled jumble with intrusive pieces of something that looks like small, sweet gum balls or some type of burr mixed with it. Top of braided end looks cut. Measuring: total length: 127 mm; braid length: 57.2 mm; braid width: 11.1 mm; braid thickness: 6.35 mm. Thread is incomplete and in poor condition. Catalog number **VICKC-1086.**

SPOOLS

Several dozen wooden spools, one still holding black thread, were salvaged. They were of a very lightweight white wood. They looked like modern-day spools. The spools varied in size.

According to Margie Bearss' records, the spools started to warp and split almost immediately after being salvaged. Several were put into strong polyethylene glycol solution. Several were treated with

Spools. VICKC-4801. Bearss numbers 4337, 4338.

plastic. Nothing seemed to work. Bearss says that the spools "all warped before our very eyes."

Seeing that they were losing them, they tried various experiments to try to preserve the spools. One was treated with a solution of 100 percent polyethylene and one was soaked in linseed oil.

Three or four are left, and they are flattened and split. They are the ones treated with plastic. Nothing can be done for these. The others are completely lost.

Two spools pictured here are catalogued **VICKC-4801**; Bearss numbers 4337, 4338.

THIMBLE

A small, pitted, ferrous metal band. The top is open. The base is wider in diameter than the top. Shiny brownish color. Measuring: height: 15.9 mm; top diameter: 17.5 mm; base diameter: 19.1 mm. Thimble is complete and in good condition. Catalog number **VICKC-1088.**

THIMBLE

A small, pitted ferrous metal band. The top is open. Small ridge around the bottom edge. The base is wider in diameter than the top. Small section of top edge has rusted away. Dark color. Light rust. Measuring: height: 19.1 mm; top diameter: 17.5 mm; base diameter: 20.6 mm. Complete but in fair condition. Catalog number **VICKC-1099.**

Thimbles. VICKC-1088 (*left*) and VICKC-1099.

NEEDLEWORK KIT

Piece of thin black leather. Rectangular shape. One end torn. Stitch holes along all four edges. Raised pattern embossed on front. Fancy scroll work. Oval section at center. Stamped in small oval at

Needlework kit. VICKC-1895.

middle is "MANUFACTURED/TO ORDER/AND WARRANTED." Back is rough. Brown areas. Original shape (folded?) unknown. Small tears along top edge. Slightly tacky. Measuring: length: 171 mm; width: 105 mm. Kit is incomplete and in poor condition. Catalog number **VICKC-1895.**

Buttons

Many small white buttons, identified as underwear buttons, were also found. Dark shirt buttons are of two types. One type is wood. Several of these have broken into pieces. The pea jacket buttons are made from hard rubber. They are made from four different molds.

The brass buttons are of several types. The large brass Navy

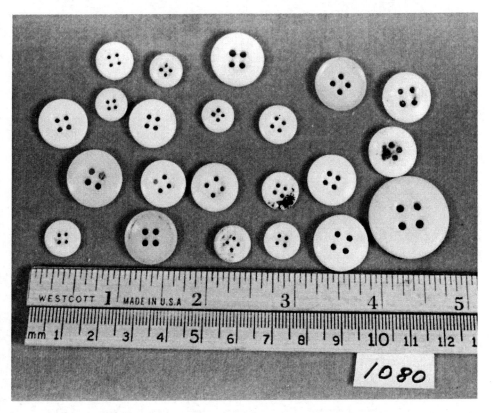

White buttons of all sizes. Bearss number 1080.

buttons are made by Scoville of Waterbury and D. Evans of Attleboro, Massachusetts. A few are made by Steele and Johnson. The medium-sized brass Navy buttons are also sturdy and in good condition.

Both the large and medium-sized buttons have eyes on the back. The tiny brass sleeve buttons evidently had very cheap tin backs.

Other than the regulation Navy buttons there are:
- Massachusetts Militia buttons
- Infantry buttons (I on shield)
- Staff officers' buttons (stripes on shield)
- Cavalry buttons (C on shield)

There was one shoe button. Several different types of small 4-eyed metal coverall buttons made by several companies. One was made by Peter Maples & Co., Philadelphia. A few were made by James H. Boyd, New York. These were painted black. There were three or four types without any manufacturer's name.

There were two buttons with cloth covering made from a navy blue covering.

BUTTON

Brass Sanders-type U.S. Navy button. Button is back marked "D. EVANS & CO. ATTLEBORO MASS." On the front in relief is a lined field with an eagle quartering to the left with head to left and wings raised. Right foot is on stock and left on shank of an almost horizontal anchor with flukes to the left. Three cannonballs below with thirteen 5-pointed stars encircling. All within a circle of cable which passes through anchor ring. Measuring: Diameter: 22.2 mm. The position of the upper fluke of the anchor, behind the eagle's wing, indicates that this button was manufac-

Button, brass Sanders type. VICKC-590.

tured between 1848 and 1859. Button is complete and in good condition. Catalog number **VICKC-590.**

U.S. Navy Enlisted Man's Pea Coat Buttons

U.S. Navy enlisted man's pea coat buttons. Made of hard rubber, black. The front of each button has a raised rim and a concave stippled field with no raised rims around the four holes. A 5-pointed star is at the center and one is on each side (3 total). "U.S.N." is printed above and a horizontal fouled anchor with flukes. On the opposite side is written "NOVELTY RUBBER Co./GOODYEAR'S PATENT./1851/NEW YORK." Measuring: diameter: 1⅜" (34.9 mm); thickness: ³⁄₁₆" (4.76 mm). Buttons are in good condition. Bearss number 1408.

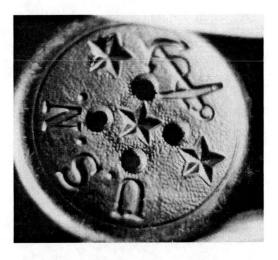

U.S. Navy enlisted pea coat button made of hard rubber (front view). VICKC-1119. Bearss number 1408.

U.S. Navy enlisted pea coat buttons made of hard rubber. *Left:* obverse view featuring patent information. *Right:* front view.

BUTTONS

White buttons made of bone. Four-eyed buttons with concave center on one side. Some darkly stained with unknown brown substance, adhering to side surface. Eye holes encrusted with brown substance. Measuring: thickness: 0.3cm; diameter: 1.5 cm (irregular).

White bone buttons. VICKC-2970.

Close-up of buttons VICKC-2970.

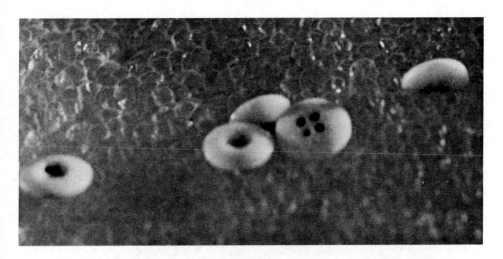

White bone buttons. VICKC-2967.

Buttons are complete and in excellent condition. Catalog number (for the lot) **VICKC-2970**.

BUTTONS

White buttons made of bone. Four-eyed buttons with concave center on one side. Some rust stains. Eye holes of some encrusted with dark unknown substance. Measuring: Thickness: 0.2 cm, Diameter: 1 cm (irregular). Buttons are complete and in excellent condition. Catalog number (for the lot) **VICKC-2967**.

Leather Articles

When the final artifacts came up to Vicksburg from Ingalls in 1960, the artifacts committee was faced with the problem of treatment of the leather articles. When the leather objects first were salvaged they were intact and supple after the mud was washed off. There was much unused leather—shoes and so forth—which came from the quartermaster's commissary storeroom. The shoes were stored in burlap bags. There were three types of shoes on board but only one type unused in the storeroom—evidently Navy issue (examples, **VICKC-1906** and **VICKC-1907**, are pictured.) They were high

Black leather boot for a left foot, catalog number VICKC-4658. Leather is in good condition.

topped. They had leather strings and had a regular pattern of nails on the soles—probably to keep the sailors from slipping on a wet deck. These shoes, contrary to the practice of the time, were made from different lasts for right and left feet. (A right-foot last, **VICKC-1568**, was found aboard the *Cairo* and is pictured here.)

A second type of shoe was Army issue. They had no hobnails, and had metal eyelets. Their cloth strings were machine stitched. Only one of these shoestrings was saved. These shoes had small horseshoe-type metal heel plates. These had been worn, and were not nearly so plentiful as the Navy issue.

Officers' boots were brought up intact but the threads deteriorated rapidly, the tops came apart, and the soles separated as each layer warped slightly. Then there was a completely different type—commercially manufactured shoes—civilian—made by Green & Co. The name is imprinted on several of the heels and under this is the size. One

Shoe last. VICKC-1568. Bearss number 2424. Lasts for left and right shoes were unusual for that time period. This last appears to be made for a right shoe.

Black leather Navy issue shoe, VICKC-1906, made for the right foot.

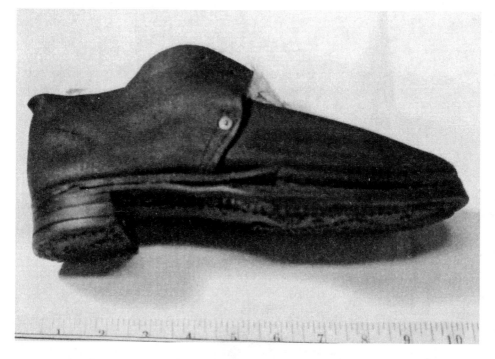

Black leather Navy issue shoe, VICKC-1907, made for the left foot.

in the museum can be found with a size 8 imprinted on it. These shoes are for men, women, and children. The explanation for these shoes was simple. Near Memphis, the *Cairo* had captured a Confederate steamboat carrying a cargo of shoes.

The Navy issue shoes were found in the commissary storeroom, the Army shoes and the civilian shoes and the few officers' boots were found in all parts of the vessel.

During the first few weeks out of the water the threads, which were already rotten when they came up, completely disintegrated. Thus the rare powder-passing boxes with "USNY Boston" stamped on their bottoms, the thumbstalls, the fuze boxes, cartridge boxes (some made in New Orleans, some regular Army issue with the car-tridge box ornaments marked "U. S.") are all in pieces. A cartridge box and 3 cap pouches have been resewn and are as good as new.

Several leather belts were found—one still showing which notch it had been fastened in.

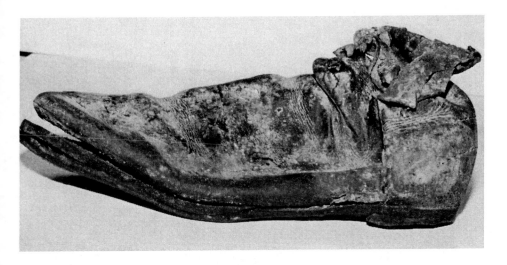

Shoe. VICKC-4437.

SHOES

Leather shoe bears: "SHOE/COMMERCIAL" Almost all of shoe intact. Left, square-toe man's boot—top deteriorated. Heel missing with some remnant of heel. Bottom appears to have been very greasy. Covered with silt. Measuring: length: 26.5 cm; width (at toe): 9 cm. Shoe is complete and in fair condition. Catalog number **VICKC-4437.**

SHOE HEEL

Bearss: "crudely made heel" (with side view showing layers uneven) however, detailing around top and precision of edges and shape suggests only damaged by water. Heel appears to be made of leather. Measuring: length: 6 cm; width: 6 cm; diameter: (approximately) 3 cm. Fragment is in poor condition. Catalog number **VICKC-4438.**

Shoe heel. VICKC-4438.

8

PERSONAL EFFECTS

Toiletries and Personal Care Items

COMB

Black hard rubber comb. Shiny. The back of the comb is curved with the widest part of the comb being over the longest teeth. Half of the comb is made of small fine teeth of uniform size. The other half is made of large teeth of various lengths depending on their position in the curve. The teeth are flat, coming to a point at the end. Imprinted on the comb in small letters on one side is "I.R. COMB Co. GOODYEAR'S_PATENT MAY 6, 1851." On the other side is printed "U.S. NAVY." Small area of white paint on small teeth on one side. Measuring: length: 171 mm; width (maximum) 47.6 mm; width (minimum) 34.9 mm; thickness: 4.76 mm. Comb is complete and in good condition. Catalog number **VICKC-1600**.

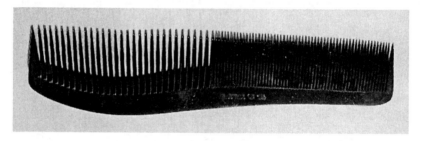

Comb. VICKC-1600.

COMB

Black hard rubber comb. The back of the comb is curved with the widest part of the comb being over the longest teeth. Half of the comb is made up of small fine teeth nearly uniform in length. The other half is made of large teeth of different lengths, getting progressively longer at the widest part of the comb and shorter again toward the end. The teeth are flat, coming to a point at the end. One side has imprinted in small letters: "I.R. COMB Co GOODYEAR'S / PATENT MAY 6, 1851." On the opposite side is imprinted in large letters "U.S. NAVY." Measuring: length: 6¹³⁄₁₆" (173 mm); narrowest width: 1½" (31.8 mm); widest width: 1¹³⁄₁₆" (46 mm); thickness: ³⁄₁₆" (4.76 mm). Comb is in good condition. Catalog number **VICKC-346**.

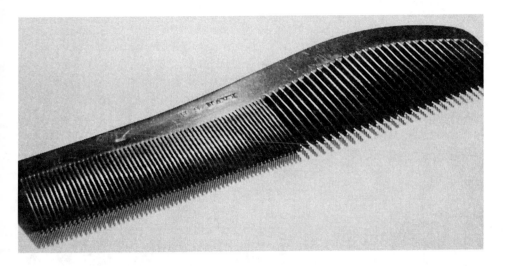

Comb. VICKC-346.

HAIRBRUSH

Long-handled hairbrush with back and handle. Made of two pieces of wood. Both are flat and relatively thin with bottom piece being thickest. Top piece fits on top of bottom piece and is of the same shape except of smaller dimension. Both pieces are shiny (lac-

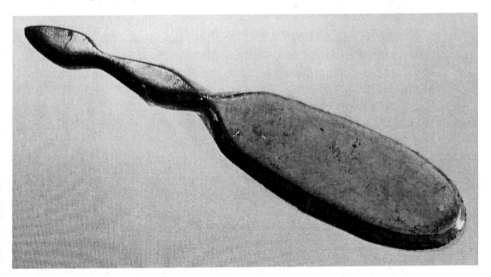

Hairbrush. VICKC-381.

Hairbrush. VICKC-1813.

quered?). Back of brush is oval shaped, tapering toward the handle. The handle is narrow, elongated figure-eight shape. Back of top piece is painted a tan color. Paint mostly worn off handle. Piece beneath is of a slightly darker brown color. Opposite side black. No bristles or holes for bristles. Measuring: length: 276 mm; back width: 63.5 mm. Hairbrush is incomplete but in fair condition. Catalog number **VICKC-381.**

HAIRBRUSH

Made of wood in one piece, which makes up the back and handle. Thin. Front side is a natural, wood color. The layer the bristles fit into is missing. Small nail holes all around edges. Hole through end of handle. Back has light brown or cream colored original paint on it. Shape is wide at the top, narrowing to the throat, getting wider for handle. Slightly warped. Heavily lacquered. Measuring: length: 257 mm; thickness: 3.18 mm; maximum width: 76.3 mm. Hairbrush is incomplete but in good condition. Catalog number **VICKC-1813.**

MIRRORS

The mirrors had about half the reflecting surface still on when recovered. This surface began to peel as soon as it dried. One small rectangular mirror (brass framed) from the pilot house was untreated from the time it was salvaged in 1960 until 1964. Almost all the reflecting surface was gone when it was brought into the workshop.

Seeing that something had to be done to save the mirrors, Margie Bearss tried spraying the back with clear plastic. This did not change the appearance of the mirrors any and seemed to help with this object's long-term preservation.

MIRROR

Rectangular mirror with no frame. Silvering is in good condition. One small clear spot. Numerous flaws on spots in the silvering but still presents a good reflection. A few cloudy areas on the surface. Flaws in glass along one edge. Measuring: length: 6⁵⁄₁₆" (160 mm); width: 4½" (114 mm); thickness: ¼" (6.35 mm). Mirror is in good condition. Catalog number **VICKC-1023**.

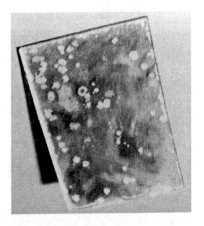

Mirror. VICKC-1023.

MIRROR

Oval mirror with a fancy brass frame. The mirror is broken in 4 pieces. The silvering is good, except for small spots and damage along one edge. The frame has a raised pattern around the top edge and the outer rim has a smaller

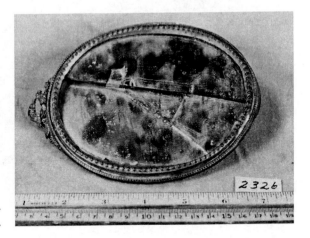

Mirror. VICKC-1024.
Bearss number 2326.

pattern. Top edge has a fancy piece of brass with a hole in it so mirror could be hung. This is not bent. The back is made of tin, with the brass edge bent down over it. The tin is a dark brown, rusty, with 2 raised ridges forming circles at the center. Mirror is in fair condition. Measuring: total length: 6½" (165 mm); width: 4⅞" (124 mm). Catalog number **VICKC-1024**.

SOAP CRATE FRAGMENT

Rectangular piece of wood. One complete side of a crate. Nail holes along all 4 sides. One sticking out of the top. Stenciled in black ink is "PALM SOAP/GOODWIN & ANDERSON/60 lbs." Measuring: length: 13⅜" (340 mm); width: 9½" (241 mm); thickness: ¹³⁄₁₆" (20.6 mm). Overall condition is good. Wood has a waxy surface due to preservation with PEG. Catalog number **VICKC-1026**.

Soap crate fragment. VICKC-1026.

SOAP

Large chunk of white pow-
dered soap. Outside: white with
numerous light brown spots.
Measuring: length: 197 mm;
width: 102 mm; thickness: 57.2
mm. Overall condition of soap is
good. Catalog number **VICKC-
1417.**

Soap. VICKC-1417.

WASHING PITCHER

Washing pitcher. VICKC-332.

Washing pitcher. VICKC-330.

Large, fancy, white china pitcher. Finish very good. Ten facets. Base creates foot effect. Angles outward. Body rounds upward. At widest point meets upper body at angle. Two ridges at this point. Facets taper gradually up to flared mouth edge which is thick and grooved. Fancy handle has leaf-shaped design on top and inside. Underside of base has wide unglazed edge. Recessed center. Ten-sided, dark green hard glob of unknown substance on basal edge. Pitcher is complete and in good condition. Measuring: height: 30.3 cm; width:

Washing pitcher. VICKC-334.

20.3 cm; base diameter: 13.7 cm. Catalog number **VICKC-332.**
Found with bowl catalog number **VICKC-331.**

WASHING PITCHER

Large, fancy, white china pitcher. Crazed base angles out from
body. Footed effect. Body rounded with 7 facets created by indenta-
tions. Facets widen up to widest part of body (angled) then narrow
up to flared mouth, where they widen. Pouring spout is taller than
handle side. Handle is light with fancy scroll design. Attached at
mouth top and on body just above widest part. Base deeply recessed
and flat. Pitcher relatively lightweight, stands on unglazed ridge.
Pitcher is complete but in fair condition. Measuring: height: 23.8 cm;
width: 15.9 cm; base diameter: 11.4 cm. Catalog number **VICKC-
334.**

WASHING PITCHER

Large, plain, white china pitcher. Heavy. Finish good. Few crazing lines on inside (yellow), few on base. Main part rounded. Tapers
up toward mouth, which flares out. Top edge has thick groove wide,
angular handle, heavy, attached below rim and above wide part of
body. Mold mark down both sides and on handle. Thick base, bottom slightly recessed, wide unglazed edge. Printed in black near base
edge: "J.J. BROWN/IMPORTER/NEW ALBANY/INDIANA." Measuring: height: 27.3 cm; base diameter: 11.4 cm. Pitcher is complete
and in good condition. Found standing upright in pilot house. Catalog number **VICKC-330**.

WASHING BOWL

Large, round, white china washbowl from pilot house. Plain with
crazing. Sides slope broadly upward. Relatively narrow rim, groove
around edge. Base is convex. Stamped at center in black letters is "J.J.
BROWN/IMPORTER/NEW ALBANY/INDIANA." Ridge around

Washing bowl. VICKC-329.

outside edge of base which bowl stands on. No chips or cracks in bowl. Crazing on base has taken on gray color. Some gray lines on inside as well as numerous faint brown stains. Rust-colored stain on rim. Measuring: height: 10.8 cm; top diameter: 34.9 cm; base diameter: 18.9 cm. Washbowl is complete and in good condition. Catalog number **VICKC-329.**

TOOTHBRUSH

Wooden toothbrush. Handle's edges and top are rounded. The head has angular edges. The handle narrows toward the end. The back is curved upward (warped?). Uneven brown paint, some of it worn off. Has shiny finish. Narrow neck. Head has 4 rows of tiny holes (22 holes per row) to hold bristles. No bristles extant. It narrows at the top. The top is rounded. Measuring: length: 6¼" (159 mm); width of handle: ½" (12.7 mm). Toothbrush is incomplete but in good condition. Catalog number **VICKC-351.** Bearss number 5601.

TOOTHBRUSH

Wooden toothbrush. Handle's edges and top are rounded. The handle is arched somewhat and flattens toward the end. The neck is narrow. The head narrows toward the top, which is rounded. Head has 4 rows of tiny holes to hold bristles. No bristles extant. Medium dull brown color, faint shine. Measuring: length: 6¹⁄₁₆" (154 mm); width of handle: ½" (12.7 mm). Toothbrush incomplete and in poor condition. Handle has several splits on each side. Broken in two at the neck. The back of the head is split, pieces broken. Catalog number **VICKC-1027.** Bearss number 1966.

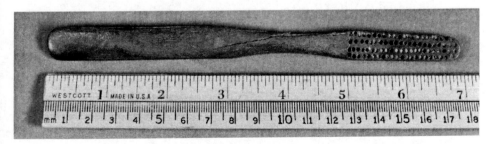

Toothbrush. VICKC-351. Bearss number 5601.

Soap dish. VICKC-325. Bearss number 2949.

SOAP DISH

Rectangular soap dish made of white ironstone china. A few crazing lines. These have taken on a yellow color. The main part of the dish is recessed about ¾" (1.905 cm) from the top edge. The sides slope outward. Two raised parallel lines at the inside corner. Four corners of dish are notched and rounded. Base is flat, recessed. Dish rests on an outer ridge. Measuring: length: 4¹⁄₁₆" (10.319 cm); width: 3⅝" (9.208 cm); height: 1⅛" (2.858 cm). Soap dish is complete and in good condition. One edge looks like it was chipped before it was glazed. Catalog number **VICKC-325.** Bearss number 2949.

SOAP DISH

Deep rectangular dish made of white china. From pilot house. Good finish, shiny, not crazed. Top rim extends out over the dish. The rim has angled edges. Corners are angled off. Center bottom has small drainage holes. Sides nearly vertical. Inside corners rounded. Under side of base slightly concave. Underneath the rim and part way down the sides the finish is unglazed. Measuring: height: 1⅝" (4.128

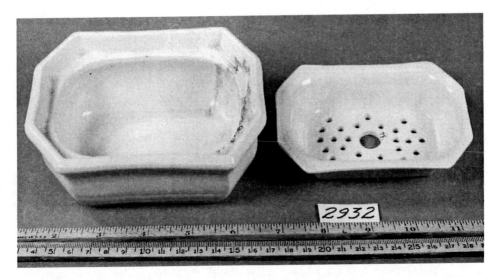

Soap dish. VICKC-326. Bearss number 2932.

Soap dish. VICKC-326 containing inner draining dish.

cm); depth: 1½" (3.810 cm); width: 3⁷⁄₁₆" (8.731 cm); length: 4⅝" (11.748 cm). Soap dish is complete and in good condition. Not chipped, cracked or broken. Catalog number **VICKC-326**. Bearss number 2932.

SHAVING BRUSH FRAGMENT

Wooden handle is badly warped, split and shrunken. It has a very narrow waist. It fits into a piece made of metal which is round and holds the bristles. This piece is wide at the top and tapers toward the bottom. It has a groove in it about ⅓ of the way down. The bristles extend out the bottom and are broken off ⁵⁄₁₆" (7.94 mm) from the holder. The handle and holder are covered with a shiny black resin. Measuring: total length: 3¹⁄₁₆" (77.8 mm); length of handle: 1⁷⁄₁₆" (36.5 mm); diameter of holder: ¹⁵⁄₁₆" (23.8 mm). Shaving brush fragment is in poor condition. Catalog number **VICKC-1021**.

RAZOR

Straight razor. Single-edge ferrous metal blade with black finish. Folds down into long wooden handle which is thin, shiny and brown. Open on both sides. One end wider than other, with brass rivet. Both ends rounded. Brass rivet at other end goes through blade handle core; blade pivots on rivet in both directions. Blade, handle core made

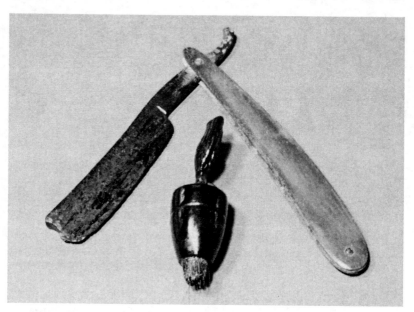

Shaving brush fragment (VICKC-1021) pictured with razor (VICKC-788).

in one piece. Blade narrows toward end. Very end turns up. End protrudes beyond wooden handle. Round notch top of blade, back flat. "Man_factured/th...el" imprinted on blade handle. Razor is complete and in good condition. Razor blade is 140 mm long and 20.6 mm wide. Handle is 140 mm long and 19.1 mm wide. Catalog number **VICKC-788**.

SAILOR'S PERSONAL CHEST

Small wooden chest in very poor, fragile condition. Held together by thin wires. Wood was thin. It has warped, split and broken. Most of the back is missing. Two small hinges still intact on the one piece of wood across the back. Some of the hardware still intact. Small metal handle standing up on lid. Tin straps with brass tacks fit over the lid on each side. Heavier ferrous metal strap along bottom edge of lid. Brass lock plate with tiny key hole and swinging hole cover.

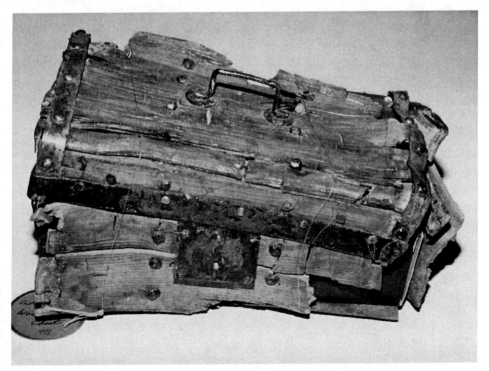

Sailor's personal chest. VICKC-1128.

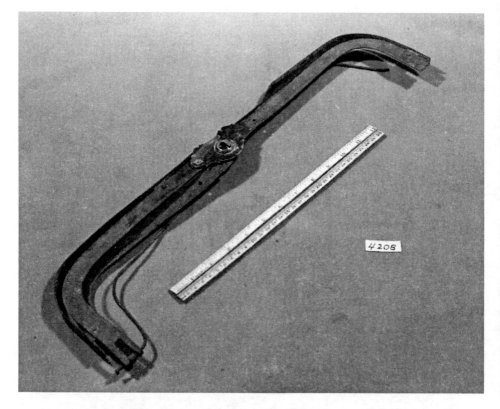

Carpetbag frame. VICKC-3396. Bearss number 4208.

Wood is a light brown. Numerous tacks still in the wood. Measuring approximately: length: 267 mm; width: 165 mm; Height: 165 mm; thickness (of wood): 11.1 mm. Chest is complete but in poor condition. Catalog number **VICKC-1128**.

CARPETBAG FRAME

Flat, rectangular ferrous metal fragment of carpetbag frame. Both ends broken at angle. One jammed. Two rectangular slots along one long edge. One has edge portion broken away. Bent and nearly split near broken slot. Thin, heavily corroded. Dark in color. Measuring: length: 27.7 cm; width: 1.9 cm; thickness: 0.1 cm. Frame is in poor condition. Catalog number **VICKC-3396**. Bearss number 4208.

Mementos

AMBROTYPE

Small rectangular piece of glass with an image on it. Pictured are a woman and a young girl, unidentified. Girl's right hand rests on woman's left shoulder. Both are wearing plaid dresses and somber expressions. Glass is enclosed in a fancy, thin brass frame. The edges

Ambrotype of woman and child. VICKC-1131.

Photograph made from ambrotype. VICKC-1131.

are folded down over the back. Inside is a fancy brass matte border with a flower design in each corner. Measuring: length: 88.9 cm; width: 69.9 cm. Complete and in fair condition. Catalog number **VICKC-1131.**

AMBROTYPE

Small, rectangular piece of glass with a faded gray negative image on it. Glass is enclosed in a fancy brass frame. The edges of the thin brass are folded down over the back. Inside is a fancy brass matte border with an open oval center. Picture of a man. Back has a tag taped on it. Tape has yellowed. Yellowed look to glass on negative. Measur-

Ambrotype of man. **VICKC-1130.**

ing: length: 63.5 cm; width: 50.8 cm; thickness: 6.35 cm. Complete but in fair condition. Found in Seaman Brown's personal chest. Identity of man unknown. Catalog number **VICKC-1130.**

Recreational Items

DOMINOES

The dominoes warped some but not much.

Sailors aboard the USS *Cairo* led rather dull lives in the fall of 1862. While they waited for orders to head down the Mississippi River, they spent long days preparing the gunboat and practicing for battle. Anxious to face Confederate forces near Vicksburg, they fought an unexpected enemy—boredom.

On the morning of November 17, Third Assistant Engineer George Aiken faced a long, hot shift watching gauges in the engine

Dominoes found on board *Cairo*. Featured in this photograph
are VICKC-428, VICKC-429, VICKC-430, VICKC-431, and VICKC-
432.

room. Captain Thomas O. Selfridge wanted to run engine tests and
needed a "working power of steam at noon." Aiken saw that the fires
were well fueled, then he opened the dampers and steam began to
build. The engineer was officially on duty, but he grew restless. Sure
that everything was in order, he decided to slip away and challenge
another sailor to a game of dominoes.

In the deserted engine room, steam pressure increased. As
George Aiken played dominoes, the temperature in the belly of the
ship reached a new high.

Andrew Lusk was just a fireman aboard *Cairo*. He was officially
off duty that morning and simply passing through when he noticed
an unusual amount of heat in the boiler room. When he checked the
steam gauge he saw the needle passing 205 pounds of pressure. He
knew if something wasn't done right away the mounting steam pressure would cause an explosion—which could spell disaster within the
confines of *Cairo*'s ironclad walls.

Lusk couldn't locate Aiken, so he ran up on deck and found
another engineer. That officer immediately made adjustments and
lowered the steam pressure. Once the situation was under control
and a level of safety restored, the search went out for George Aiken.

He was found intent over his dominoes, unaware of the tragedy just averted. The game came to an abrupt end when officers burst in and dragged Aiken forward to face his furious captain.

No one knows if George Aiken won or lost at dominoes that day. He did lose his job; Selfridge immediately suspended him from duty. Andrew Lusk was cited for his quick actions, and was eventually promoted to third assistant engineer.

DOMINO

Black. Made up of two layers of wood, one thin, one thick. Held together by a tiny nail at each end. Front very glossy, back not. The pattern is six dots on one half, blank on the other. Line drawn down the middle. Measuring: length: 36.5 mm; width: 19.1 mm; thickness: 7.94 mm. Domino is complete and in good condition. One of six found. Catalog number **VICKC-428.**

DOMINO

Black. Made up of two layers of wood, one thin, one thick. Held together by a tiny nail at each end. Front highly glossy, back is not. The pattern is two dots on one half, blank on the other. Line drawn down the middle. Measuring: length: 36.5 mm; width: 19.1 mm; thickness: 7.94 mm. Domino is complete and in good condition. One of six found. Catalog number **VICKC-429.**

DOMINO

Black. Made up of two layers of wood, one thin, one thick, tightly joined by a tiny nail at each end. Both front and back are very glossy. Pattern is three dots on one half, six dots on the other. Line drawn down the middle. Measuring: length: 36.5 mm; width: 19.1; mm, thickness: 7.94 mm. Domino is complete and in good condition. One of six found. Catalog number **VICKC-430.**

DOMINO

Black. Made up of two layers of wood, one thin, one thick. Held together by a tiny nail at each end. All sides highly glossy. The pattern is four dots on one half, blank on the other. Line drawn down the middle. Measuring: length: 36.5 mm; width: 19.1 mm; thickness: 7.94 mm. Domino is complete and in good condition. One of six found. Catalog number **VICKC-432.**

LEATHER BOOK COVERS

One book cover (leather) was thrown up by the suction pump early in the salvage operations. It was a complete leather spine cover. On it was imprinted (letters pressed in) ORRENDORF'S FRENCH GRAMMAR (on display within the museum today).

Another book cover, torn but part of a whole cover, had fancy designs. In gold was printed HOLY BIBLE. With a magnifying glass one could read "London Bible Society." This one began to shrink immediately.

Parts of two other Bible covers were found.

BOOK

Made of very thin black leather. Outline of the shape of the back of the book can be seen as ridges on the flat piece of leather which includes the overlapping edges. Also 4 horizontal ridges spaced on the spine. Original gold lettering was lost during preservation treat-

Black leather book fragment. VICKC-1144. Bearss number 1866.

ment. According to the original catalog it read: "ORRENDORF_FRENCH_GRAMMAR." Measuring: total length: 181 mm; total width: 68.3 mm. Book fragment is in poor condition. Catalog number **VICKC-1144.** Bearss number 1866.

Carving (Star)

Wood carving. Small, long cylindrical piece of wood. One end has been very neatly carved to make a 5-pointed star stamp. The other end is flat with a carved edge. The star is stained black from ink. Spot of ink on the side. Measuring: length: 55.6 cm; diameter: 17.5 mm. Catalog number **VICKC-392.**

Wood carving in shape of 5-pointed star. VICKC-392.

Carving

Semicircular wood carving. Other half not located. Flat bottom. Inside split runs from top to bottom. Top has 12 ridges cut out resembling sunburst. Grain of wood visible on split area. Wood "oily" and flaky. Dark brown in color. Measuring: height: 5.0 cm; diameter: 5.9 cm. Carving is incomplete but in fair condition. Catalog number **VICKC-2605.**

Carving (Boat)

Hull of a boat carved from soft pine wood. The top is flat. The bow comes to a point. The stern is rounded. The sides slant downward to

Boat carving. VICKC-561.

the keel. The wood is brown, soft to the touch and somewhat tacky. Measuring: length: 229.0 mm; width: 74.6 mm. Carving is complete and in good condition. Catalog number **VICKC-561.**

Jewelry and Timepieces

A large assortment of jewelry was found among the artifacts recovered from the sunken ironclad. Timepieces were also found.

Included among the items:

• Selfridge's oak leaf—It is in good condition.
• A stick pin with an eagle sitting on a flag-draped globe. This appears to be made from inexpensive metal. According to Margie Bearss' records, it looked as if it had been burned or possibly suffered some oxidation.

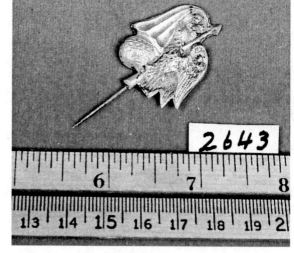

• A snake bracelet. There was a link bracelet with a snake's head. It had a small dangling locket about half an inch in diameter. The locket has no fastener, and is empty.
• A cluster of lavender beads—each on a brass ring and all linked together.

Eagle stick pin. VICKC-1138. Bearss number 2643.

• Hand-carved wooden ring. This ring was carved of some type of dark and very hard wood.
• Two watches.
• A bracelet made of leather, edged on both sides by a narrow band of what may be gold.
• Another ring, possibly a wedding ring or simply a ring from a musical instrument.

POCKET WATCH

Small pocket watch with a round brass case. The face, glass, and hands are gone. Some of the inner works are still intact. Rusty layered surface which would have been the part behind the face is now visible. A small handle on top for a chain. Brass quite tarnished. Many parts gone. Measuring: diameter (of case): 49.2 mm; thickness: 12.7 mm. The watch is incomplete and in poor condition. According to Margie Bearss' records, it was the second watch brought up. Catalog number VICKC-1135.

Pocket watch. VICKC-1135.

POCKET WATCH

Pocket watch. VICKC-1558.

Pocket watch. VICKC-1558. (view of outer case).

This was the first of two watches found. The worker who opened the watch case did not notice at what time the watch had stopped. By the time it was brought into the workshop the hands had been moved.

It was taken to a local repairman, who sent it to an antique watch specialist. Mr. H. V. Cooper, chairman of the *Cairo* committee, authorized it to be fixed. New parts were made—some minute links of a chain-like mechanism were handmade. A new glass was put on. The cost of $126 was paid by the Vicksburg Chamber of Commerce. The watch was restored to working order.

Silver (?) case. Roman numerals. Face has "RAILWAY TIME-KEEPER" printed in red at top over "JOS JOHNSON/LIVERPOOL." Front and back hinged, will open and close. Name "Callihan" scratched on it. Inside back is a peg for winding. Two keys, one original and one made. Inside case restored (in 1960s, probably after salvage) by James D. Cannon, according to Mrs. Bearss. He described watch as a Crown Wheel verge escapement, fusee chain-driven watch. Measuring: diameter (of case): 58.7 mm; thickness: 20.6 mm. Catalog number **VICKC-1558**.

POCKET WATCH CHAIN

Brass watch chain in the shape of a snake. Individual round brass segments linked together make up the body. The segments are widest in diameter at the middle and taper toward the head and tail. End of tail is not segmented but forms a small loop. Snake head has seam along top and bottom. In his open mouth was made a small brass ring. This has another ring added on it. To the second ring is attached a small piece of brass with a loop at each end. Top loop is broken. Attached to bottom loop is an ornament (?) which looks like a miniature brass watch (?) made in two halves, now slightly separated. Measuring: length: 305 mm; length (of head): 4.76 mm; diameter (at widest part of the body): 4.76 mm. Chain is complete and in good condition. Catalog number **VICKC-1137**. Bearss number 2662.

Pocket watch chain. VICKC-1137. Bearss number 2662.

OCCUPATIONAL PIN
(SELFRIDGE'S STICK PIN)

Brass, very thin, light. Looks like it was made in a mold in the shape of three leaves and acorns. Brass is a shiny golden color with brown tarnish in cracks and on edges. Back has a long straight pin and catch. Measuring: length: 47.6 mm; width: 30.2 mm. Pin is complete and in good condition. Catalog number **VICKC-1791**. Bearss number 2644.

Occupational pin (Selfridge's stick pin) VICKC-1791. Bearss number 2644.

LAVENDER BEADS

Three lavender beads on interlocking rings. Round lavender beads have tiny brown flecks. Each bead has a round metal piece with a small loop on it for which to fasten the bead to the round metal ring. One bead is slightly chipped. White areas around the chips and large brown flecks. Another bead is lightly pitted, white in these areas. The three rings interlock. Measuring: bead

Lavender beads. VICKC-327. Bearss number 1709.

diameter: 11.0 mm; ring diameter: 11.0 mm. Beads are complete and in good condition. Catalog number **VICKC-327**. Bearss number 1709.

Writing Instruments

NAME STAMP

Roughly rectangular piece of wood. Hard with dark brown natural color. Heavily lacquered, shiny. Hand carved. The sides have been rounded and the end carved to a 4-sided point at one end. Measuring: length: 137 mm; width: 12.7 mm; thickness: 19.1 mm. Name stamp is complete and in good condition. Catalog number **VICKC-425**. Bearss number 2111.

Name stamp. VICKC-425.

PENCILS

The pencils, made by the Faber Co., are No. 2 Medium, and when recovered came up in two pieces. The larger portion contained

Pencils. VICKC-1059 and VICKC-1053.

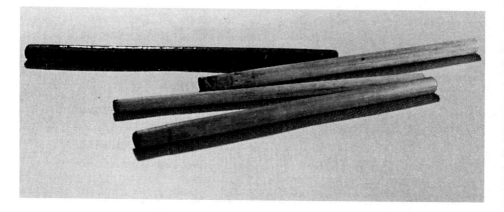

Pencils

the square lead. The only damage at all was that the substance used to glue the parts together had melted. One pencil was still sharpened and could write. A few light colored straight sticks were unidentified until one was found which had a pen point on it.

PENCIL

Made of wood. This is the piece that holds the square lead. A 57.2-mm section of lead is still extant. Pencil is round. Knife marks where it was sharpened. Wooden point is slightly broken. Other end has edges carved off. Top is flat. Dull, off-white color. Lead did not originally go to the top. Measuring: length: 133–135 mm; diameter: 7.94 mm. Pencil is complete and in good condition. Catalog number **VICKC-1059.**

PENCIL

A complete round wooden pencil. Unsharpened. Appears to be a dark green or black color underneath with an uneven cream color over this. Lacquered with a shiny appearance. Pencil made in two pieces. Large piece holds the square lead. A small piece fits down over the lead and is glued in place somewhat unevenly. Printed in very faint lettering is "...E FABER 133 WILLIAM STR. NY" Measuring: length: 176 mm; diameter: 7.94 mm. Pencil is complete and in good condition. Catalog number **VICKC-1053.**

Drawing Pens

A number of drawing pen points were brought up in good shape. At first it seemed as if they did not need any treatment, says Margie Bearss. After a few weeks the metal started to erode. Lacy holes developed in several. Within the next few days several more holes appeared. A thin coat of plastic spray was applied to several. This did not completely stop the encroachment of the holes. Several other coats were necessary.

Pen (pen points). VICKC-1064.

Pen

Made of lightweight ferrous metal. One end forms the point. Above this is a vertical slot and a line leading down to the point. The other end is round, meets at the center of the back. Black with brown areas. Heavily lacquered, shiny. May have been lacquered over rust. "RUDHALL & Co/QUILL PEN" on the front. One of 18 pen points found together. Measuring: length: 39.7 mm; diameter (of round end): 6.35 mm. Pen is complete but in fair condition. Catalog number **VICKC-1064**.

Eraser

Rectangular hard rubber eraser. Now hard and brittle. Uneven brown and tan colors with light and dark patches. Edges have faint ridges in them. Faint cracks on surface. Measuring: length: 42.9 mm; width: 34.9 mm; thickness: 11.1 mm. Eraser is complete and in good condition. Catalog number **VICKC-440**.

Eraser

Small, roughly rectangular, rubber. Black with brownish patches and small areas of white. Checking lines, fine cracks. Some wear on corners. Top and bottom are flat. Sides have ridges. It is mostly hard and brittle, but some resiliency remains. One side has two notches along the edge. Measuring: length: 28.6 mm; width: 20.6 mm; thickness: 7.94 mm. Eraser is complete and in good condition. Catalog number **VICKC-1579**.

Eraser. VICKC-1579.

SLATES

Once the slates were brought up they were placed with the rest of the artifacts recovered from *Cairo.* One unfortunate incident about their treatment was the thoroughness of their cleaning. One slate had a poem and a name written on it. Before it could be photographed, or even a note made of the inscription, it was carefully washed clean.

All that anyone can remember was that the poem began "From London to Liverpool to France—."

The name signed was "Ferguson."

CHALKBOARD (SLATE)

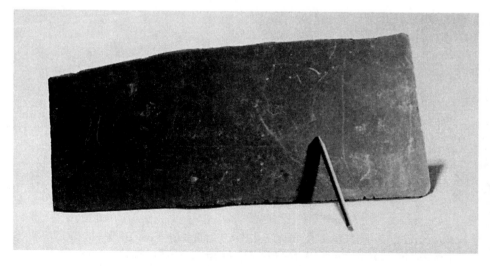

Chalkboard (slate). VICKC-3904 with slate pencil VICKC-1050.

Grayish-blue slate fragments. Some fragments are triangular shaped with jagged edges. One fragment almost perfectly rectangular with some chipped areas around the edges. All fragments contain scratches. The longest fragment has faintly written across it on one side **USS CAIRO.** Fragment is in fair condition. Catalog number **VICKC-3904.**

SLATE PENCIL

Described as a slate pencil by reference to the original catalog. Light gray slate in the shape of a small pencil. One end comes to a point. The other end is flat, uneven, appears broken. The sides are round. Covered with a white powdery substance. Measuring: length: 85.7 mm; diameter: 6.35 mm. Pencil is complete and in good condition. Catalog number **VICKC-1050.**

Antlers

Several points of a pair of antlers proved to be some of the smelliest things brought up.

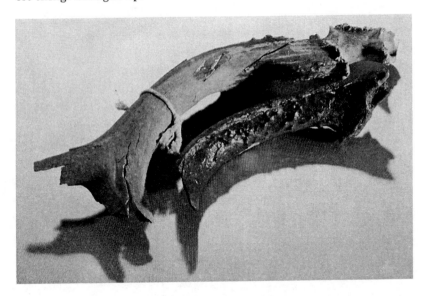

Antlers. VICKC-3052.

These antlers are interesting items of the everyday life of the sailors—showing some sailor's trophy and letting us know what the men had for one meal at least.

Two fragments of the antlers are pictured. The smaller appears to have been conserved with lacquer. Larger is untreated and has several large cracks. Both fragments are in fair condition. Measuring: longest length: 33.3 cm; width: 9.9 cm (irregular). Catalog number **VICKC-3052.**

Tobacco and Smoking Devices

Smoking was very common aboard the *Cairo*. Pipe bowls were scattered about the vessel. Clay bowls, briar bowls, and some that look like glazed porcelain were found. Divers even found blocks of tobacco.

TOBACCO

Large chunk of brown/black tobacco, made up of about (7) layers and measuring 197 mm in length × 127 mm in width × 88.9 mm

Tobacco. VICKC-1566.

in thickness. Somewhat brittle. Still has tobacco odor. Irregular shape. Complete and in good condition. Catalog number **VICKC-1566.**

Following the recovery of the tobacco, several museum experts were contacted to assist with making recommendations for its preservation. No one was able to provide much assistance. As a result some of the tobacco has powdered, deteriorated, and disintegrated. It was recommended that the tobacco be placed near dry heat. After thorough drying, the tobacco was wrapped in plastic sandwich wrap to keep the air from it and placed near the space heaters (gas) to dry.

This was the state of its preservation back in the 1960s. One block was put in a heavy solution of polyethylene glycol, but it showed no difference from the other, except that its smell is completely gone.

At this time Margie Bearss feared that the tobacco was a lost cause unless some could be sealed in airtight containers.

Today, after over 130 years, the tobacco still retains its tobacco scent due to the preservation measures that were taken by Margie in the early days, soon after its discovery. It was these early measures that helped to preserve the tobacco for today's generation.

SPITTOON

Standard army-type spittoon. Wooden with a box shape. The box rests on a square piece of wood that serves as a base. The sides

Left: Spittoon. VICKC-515. Bearss number 1727. Top view. *Right:* Bottom side view.

of the box are set in on this base about 12.7 mm from the edge. Edges of the base are slightly rounded. Four sides. Each slants outward. Box nailed together. No lid. Wood is dark. No paint or lettering. Spittoon measurements are height: 12 cm; width: 24 cm; length: 23.4 cm. In complete and good condition. Catalog number **VICKC-515**. Bearss number 1727.

PIPE BOWL

A narrow tube with a small bowl adjoining it at a right angle. Inside of bowl is round and deep, tapering toward the bottom. Blackened. Narrow rim. Made of white clay, fancy. Now a light brown with darker stains. Pattern like a flower in relief around the rim. Bowl has pattern of leaves overlapping in relief and a fancy scroll where tube and bowl join.

Mold mark. Diameter at top of bowl: 1" (25.4 mm); diameter at end of tube (broken): 5/16" (7.94 mm); length of bowl and tube: 1⅜" (34.9 mm); height of bowl: 1⅜" (34.9 mm). Pipe bowl was originally made in one piece that included stem. Stem now broken off. In good condition. Catalog number **VICKC-1031**. Bearss number 2353.

Pipe bowl. VICKC-1031. Bearss number 2353.

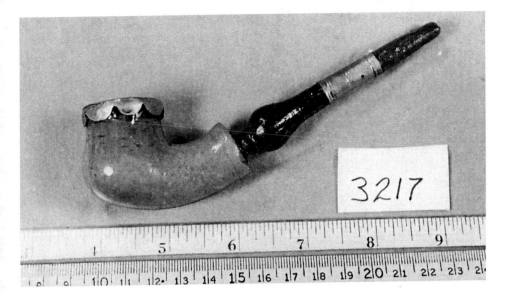

Pipe. VICKC-1033. Bearss number 3217.

PIPE

Looks like white clay "church" pipe. A narrow tube forms the short stem. It was made in one piece with the bowl. Inside of bowl is gray. It is rounded and tapers toward the bottom. Bowl is broken, has been partially mended. Large piece missing. Bowl and stem are a yellow/brownish color with many brown stains. Bowl broken, pieces missing. Some pieces glued back in. Diameter at end of stem 11.1 mm; length of bowl and stem is 87.3 mm. Catalog number **VICKC-1033**. Bearss number 3217.

PIPE BOWL

Made of some type of clay material, gray. Brown glaze is thin, gray shows through. Bowl is in shape of man's head in relief. He is wearing a turban, has a mustache. Inside of bowl is round, tapers toward bottom, not blackened. Tube adjoins bowl at right angle, is large in diameter. Mold mark. Pipe bowl in good condition. Diameter at top of bowl: 1" (25.4 mm); diameter at end of tube: ⅝" (15.9 mm); length of bowl and tube: 1⁷⁄₁₆" (36.5 mm); height of bowl: 1⁷⁄₁₆" (36.5 mm). Catalog number **VICKC-1034**.

9

MEDICAL EQUIPMENT

During *Cairo*'s raising, the medical storeroom was crushed in the salvage; consequently, only a small portion of the medical equipment was recovered.

During salvage operations, one of the divers who guided the pump head which was used to suck the mud and sand out of the vessel described what he felt while the vessel was still intact beneath the surface of the Yazoo River. During the pumping operations more than half the bottles saved were brought up by him. He found them, he said, in a small room with cabinets and counters.

Also found were

- tourniquet stops made of brass with U.S. HOSPITAL CORPS on them.
- a pill tile, broken in two pieces.
- one whole feeding dish (invalid feeder) with spout, and one that had broken into pieces.
- two ear syringes. One unscrews and has the plunger, which still works. The plunger tip is made of cotton.
- a bedpan with eagles on the back.
- sutures, which at the time of their recovery retained their elasticity. They have now been encased in plastic for their long-term preservation. The rubber bands had retained their elasticity. They were like modern rubber bands. At first glance these appeared to be hollow like tiny rubber tubes. Completely confused by them, Margie Bearss sent a sample to the Smithsonian. The answer came back, "Impossible—but these are arterial sutures."

No one knew a practical means of preserving these, so some were placed in water and some sealed in a jar.

Within a few days they began to dry and shrink. Putting them in water did not help. In panic, Margie sent some to a plastic company to be embedded in a block of plastic. Today, the block containing these sutures is on display within the Cairo Museum preserved for all to view.

All of the items listed above can now be found exhibited within the medical portion of the *Cairo* Museum.

PILL TILE

Square, flat ceramic tile. Corners are rounded. Shiny, white finish. Down approximately 31.8 mm from one edge is printed in

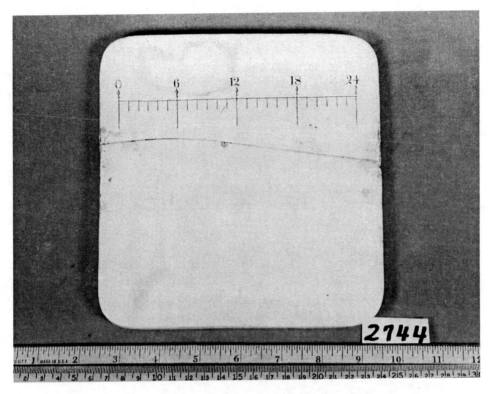

Pill tile. VICKC-1150. Bearss number 2744.

black a graduated scale of lines. The line is 152 mm long. The numbers "0, 6, 12, 18, 24" are written above the line. Five lines are marked off between each number. Broken just below the scale. Mended poorly. Excess white glue has hardened on exposed surfaces. Three light brown stains on the front. A dark band (caused by tape?) approximately 50.8 mm wide around the middle including broken area. Tape (?) has left some yellowed spots. Small chip on front bottom. Chip out of one side at the break. Measuring: length: 179 mm; width: 179 mm; thickness: 11.1 mm. Pill tile is complete and in good condition. Catalog number **VICKC-1150**. Bearss number 2744.

BEDPAN

According to the original catalog this is made of pewter. Shiny, dark gray color. Broad, flat pan. Wide round lip curves inward forming

Bedpan. VICKC-1151. Bearss number 2222. Front view.

Bedpan. VICKC-1151. Bearss number 2222. Rear view.

a partial top. There is a seam along the edge where the top edge of pan and lip section meet. Around half of the pan the seam is tight. On the other half it is coming apart. Five screws, now rusty, were put along the split. Pewter is cracked badly in two places along the edge. The large round handle screws onto the pan. Two small eagles are stamped on the back. Numerous scratches on the back. Measuring: diameter (of bottom): 254mm; diameter (of top): 181mm; length (of handle): 116mm. Bedpan is complete and in good condition. Catalog number **VICKC-1151.** Bearss number 2222.

EAR SYRINGE

Made of a gray silver-like non-ferrous metal. A long tube with a narrow cone-shaped tip. Tube has decorative grooves around the top and bottom edges. A fancy decorative band around the middle. A top, which originally screwed off and on, is wider in diameter than the tube. A hole at the top center holds a plunger which will still go up and down. A ring handle for top of plunger. Some dirt. Light and dark gray color in patches. Measuring; Length: 130mm, Maximum Diameter 19.2 mm. Syringe is complete and in good condition. Catalog number **VICKC-1146.** Bearss number 1876.

Ear syringe. VICKC-1146. Bearss number 1876.

EAR SYRINGE

Made of a gray, silver-like nonferrous metal. A long tube with a narrow cone-shaped tip. Tube has small decorative grooves around the top and bottom edges. A fancy, decorative band around the middle. A top, which originally screwed off and on, is wider in diameter than the tube. A hole at the top center holds a plunger which will now go up and down only partway. A ring handle for top of plunger. Very minor dents. Measuring: length 130 mm; maximum diameter: 19.1 mm. Syringe is complete and in good condition. Catalog number **VICKC-1147.**

FOOT TUB

Oval tub, made of some type of tin. Seam down each end, where bottom joins sides. Flat handles made of same type tin soldered on at each end. Top edge turned down over wire rim. Sides not straight, have ridge in them, taper gradually inward toward bottom. Bottom

Foot tub (side view). VICKC-875.

Foot tub (top view). VICKC-875.

nearly completely rusted out along edges. Other holes in bottom, many small holes, rust on sides. Measuring: length 362 mm; width 283 mm. Foot tub is complete but in poor condition. Found in pilot house. Catalog number **VICKC-875.**

SUTURES

Rubber suture embedded in block of clear plastic. A rectangular silver-colored metal tag also embedded in the plastic has engraved on it "U.S.S. CAIRO." The suture is brownish-black in color, thin, made in one long piece. Surface looks like it has

Sutures. VICKC-464.

tiny bumps on it. Measuring: width: 1.59 mm. Suture is complete and in good condition. Sutures were put in plastic, according to Margie Bearss, as a last resort to keep them from disintegrating. Catalog number **VICKC-464.**

INVALID CUP

Feeding dish for the sick. Small, oval, white china dish with rounded sides which taper toward base. Only half of the top is open. Other half covered in pattern of dished depressions. This side tapers outward to form neck of spout which is in the form of an animal's neck and head. Its mouth serves as the spout, with 2 eyes and a bump on top of head. Handle broken off opposite side. Base recessed, oval shaped. Finish crazed. Some dark lines and stained areas. Measuring: height: 4.1 cm; length: 12.7 cm; mouth diameter: 8.3 cm. Feeding dish is incomplete but in good condition. Catalog number **VICKC-321.** Bearss number 2317.

Invalid cup. VICKC-321. Bearss number 2317.

10

TOOLS AND
MEASURING DEVICES

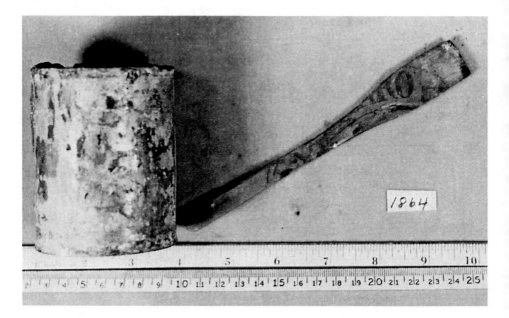

Can of blue paint (VICKC-1505) with paddle (VICKC-1506).
Together: Bearss number 1864.

CAN OF BLUE PAINT WITH PADDLE

Among the items found on *Cairo* was a small can of blue paint.
The can of paint contained a hand-made paddle that had been cut
from a cigar box top. The paint has not faded in color. This blue
paint could have been turned over during the explosion of the torpedo as evidenced by the fact that several knives and two razors, when
recovered, had traces of blue paint on them. Paint catalog number
VICKC-1505. Paddle is catalog number **VICKC-1506**. The two
together are Bearss number 1864.

A small metal container of red paint also was found. The red
faded almost immediately from a bright red to a powdery pink.

SCALES AND WEIGHTS

There were three scales and a series of weights. There were
different types of weights and several of them had one, two, or three
of the holes in the bottom plugged with lead, evidently to change
their weight.

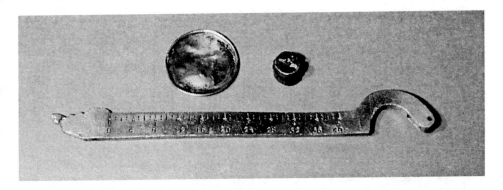

Bottom: Scale arm; *top left:* balance plate. VICKC-1149. *Top right:* balance weight. VICKC-442.

SCALE

Made of brass. Heavy. This is the end that holds the weights. It is long and flat. One end is an irregular shape with several large notches in it. The other end is a rounded hook. The top of the hook has a slot in it. The top edge of the arm has uniform notches in it. The bottom edge is smooth. On both sides of the arm are identical lines and numbers. The numbers on one scale go consecutively from 0–5. Below this the numbers go from 0–40 by fours. Tarnished. Measuring: length: 316 mm; width: 27.0 mm; thickness: 11.1 mm. Scale is incomplete but in good condition. Catalog number **VICKC-1149.**

BALANCE WEIGHT

Small metal weight, rather crudely made. Roughly round with flat top and bottom. Vertical cut in the side (formed while still molten). Material from the cut not trimmed off but forms bumps on the top. Rough uneven seam around the side. Top smaller in diameter than the bottom. Measuring: thickness: 19.1 mm; diameter: 27.0 mm. Weight is complete and in good condition. Catalog number **VICKC-442.**

SCALE

Brass scale arm. Has "PITTSBURGH NOVELTY WORKS" imprinted on one side, on the other "LIVINGSTON COPELAND

Overall view of scale VICKC-5131.

Close up view of scale end featuring two stirrup-shaped attachments.

& CO." At one end, there is a threaded iron rod (length, 10.3 cm; thickness 0.8 cm) supported by a crescent-shaped fitting at end of scale arm. There is an iron dial (diameter 4 cm) which would have screwed back and forth along the bar for fine-tuning adjustment. There are two stirrup-shaped attachments, both iron (length, 7.6 cm;

thickness 0.7 cm). Attached to posts (length, 2 cm) on either side of the arm. Along the edge at this end, "XIIII, XIII" and a pattern of three dots have been imprinted on the brass just above one of the stirrup attachments. The number "9" is imprinted at the other end. Measuring: length, 58 cm. Scale arm is incomplete but in good condition. Catalog number **VICKC-5131.**

FOLDING RULER

Wooden folding ruler with brass end pieces and hinges. Now broken in four pieces. Wood is thin, stained a dark color on 3 of the 4 pieces. Somewhat warped, checked. Marked off in sixteenths of an inch. One piece still light in color. Each side has numbers on it. Measures 584 mm in length, 15.9 mm in width with a thickness of 4.76 mm. Catalog number **VICKC-421.**

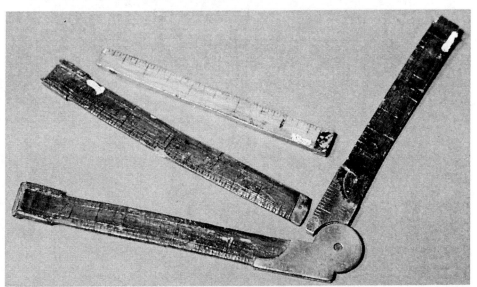

Folding ruler. VICKC-421.

OIL CAN

Made of tinned iron. Shaped like an inverted funnel. One vertical seam down the side underneath the handle. Handle is rounded, large. The top is cylindrical and has a round cap on it. The spout is

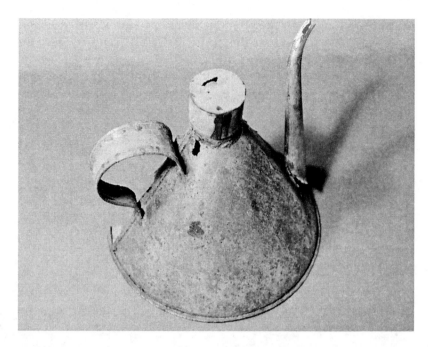

Intact side view of oil can. VICKC-460.

Opposite side view of oil can. VICKC-460.

long and slender, tapering toward the end. The bottom piece is a flat circle. Inside has a yellowish-white substance clinging to the side. Oil can bottom has a bottom diameter of 6¾", a top diameter of 1⁷⁄₁₆", a maximum width of 7½". Condition is fair. From one side it looks good. The other is poor; large pieces of tin missing from side and bottom. Spout loose. Catalog number **VICKC-460**.

GLUEPOT

Clear, transparent glass. Sides have eight facets, slanting inward toward top. Rounded ridge at top of facets, then rounded shoulder. Neck cylindrical, top edge rough. Slightly chipped. Mold mark down each side. Bottom edge round, bottom of pot dished with rounded nub of glass in center. Brush made as part of gray metal cap. Handle extends through hole in cap. Brush handle appears to be brass with rounded hook at top. Flat piece of metal bent together at end holds bristles, which are brown, soft. Measuring: height: 93.7 mm; diameter: 63.5 mm (irregular). Catalog number **VICKC-1268**.

Gluepot. VICKC-1268. Bearss number 1874.

Index

ambrotype 151–153
ammunition boxes 40–42
Anaconda Plan 5
antlers (fragments, problematic) 167–168
anvil 62–63

baking pan 96–97
barrel 100–102; half 102
base, lamp 78–79
beads, lavender 158, 162
Bearss, Edwin 9
Bearss, Margie Riddle 1–3, 15
bed frame 71
bedpan 175–177
bell: ship's 65–67; signal 58–59
book (spine—"Orrendorf French Grammar") 156–157
bottle, cathedral 108–109
bottles, condiment, Dr. Forsha's Alterative Balm, E.R. Squibb Medicine, soda pop (J. H. KUMP), worcestershire (LEA & PERRINS) 103–112
box, ammunition 40–42
bracelet 158
brush, shaving (fragment) 148
buttons 114, 125–129

Cairo discovery and salvage 9–12
Cairo restoration 12
Cairo sinking 7–9

Cairo time capsule 1, 13
Canada 6
candles (fragments) 79–80
Canizaro, Vincent 3
cannons 22–36
carriage, cannon 23–36
carving 157–158; boat 157–158; star 157
chain, pocket watch 158, 161
chair: folding (fragment) 70–71; rocking (fragment) 70
chalkboard (slate) 166–167
Chandler, Sam W. 90
chest: ice 84–85; mess 89–90; sailor's personal 149–150
City Class 5
Civil War 5, 8
cloth (fragment) 120–121
clothing and fabric 113–125
coat sleeve 119–120
coffeepot 88–89
comb 136–137
commode bowl 72–73
compass 57
Confederates 1, 9
cookware and eating utensils 83–102
cover, book (leather) 156– 157
crate fragment 65
crate, soap (fragment) 140
cups, measuring, mess 98–100

decanter 111–112
Denmark 6
direct sighting bars 38–40
dominoes 153–156
door 63–64
drawing pens 165

Eads, James Buchanan 5
England 6
eraser 165–166

fathoms 9
faucet 74–75
firebox (fragment) 64
firing mechanism 36–38
fixtures 72–75
flask, powder, priming 52–53
flotilla 8
foot tub 178–179
frame, carpetbag 150
France 6
friction primer and box 50–51
furniture 13, 69–71

Germany 6
glass, wine (fragment) 98
gluepot 187
Grabau, Warren 2, 10

hairbrush 137–138
hammock 6
hardtack 6
Hart, Skeeter 15
hatband, ribbon 13–118
hatch, door 63
heel, shoe 133

Hill, Peter Ole 95
Holy Bible 156
hydrometer 56–57

ice chest 84–85
Ingalls Shipyard 12, 15
invalid cup (feeding cup) 180
Ireland 6
ironstone 92–93

Jacks, Don 2, 9
jewelry 158–163

kit, needlework, sewing 13, 124–125

lamp base (fragment) 78–79
lamp globes 75–77
lantern and lamp globes 75–81
lantern, signal 80–81
leather articles 129–133
lighting devices 75–81
London Bible Society 156

map paper 59–60
medical equipment 173–180
mirror 139–140
Mississippi River 5
mold, bullet 53
Mound City 5
musket 44–46

name stamp 163
National Park Service 12
navigational devices 55
neckerchief 115–117
Norway 6

occupational pin (Self-ridge's Stick Pin) 158, 162
Ohio River 5
oil can 185–187
"Operation Cairo" 11, 13
Orrendorf French Grammar 14, 156–157

paddlewheel 8, 72
paint 182
pan, baking, pie 87, 96–97
Parks, Ken 3, 8, 14–15, 109
Pascagoula, MS 12
pencils 163–164; slate 167
pens 165
pepper 107–108
pepper sauce 109
pepperbox pistol 48–49
personal effects 135–171
pie pan 87
pill tile 174–175
pilot house 10, 14, 15, 22
pin: occupational (Self-ridge's Stick Pin) 158–162; rolling 86–87
pipe 171
pipe bowl 170–171
pipe, shower 72
pistol 13, 47–49
pitcher: serving (copper) 92; washing 141–144
plate, ironstone, mess 91–93
pocket watch 158, 159–160
Pook, Samuel M. 5
Pook's Turtles 5
pumps, "Hollow Tree" 65

Queen of the West 9

razor 148–149
recreational items 153–156
revolver 46–47, 48–50
rolling pin 86–87
ruler, folding 185

scales and weights 182–185
Scott, Winfield 5
Selfridge, Thomas O. 6–9, 46–47
sewing needle 121–122
ship's components 55–67

shoes 129–133
sight, military 38
signal board 57–58
signal lantern 80–81
sinking 7
slates 166–167
small arms 43–53
smoking devices 168
soap 13, 141
soap dish 146–147
"Southern Belle" cooking range 85–86
spittoon 169–170
sponges 95–96
spools 122–123
spoon 94–95
steam gauge 60–61
strongbox (safe) 61–62
sutures 179–180
syringes, ear 177–178

tea kettle (copper) 97
thimble 123–124
thread 122
tobacco 168–169
toilet 72–73
toiletries and personal care items 136–149
toothbrush 145
torpedo 8
trimmer, wick 81
tub, foot 178–179

vest 118–119
Vicksburg National Cemetery 12
Vicksburg National Military Park 9, 12, 15

washing bowl 144–145
watches 158, 159–160
Warren County (MS) 11
weight, balance 183
white oak 23
writing instruments 163–167

Yazoo River 7–9